JACKPOT TRAIL

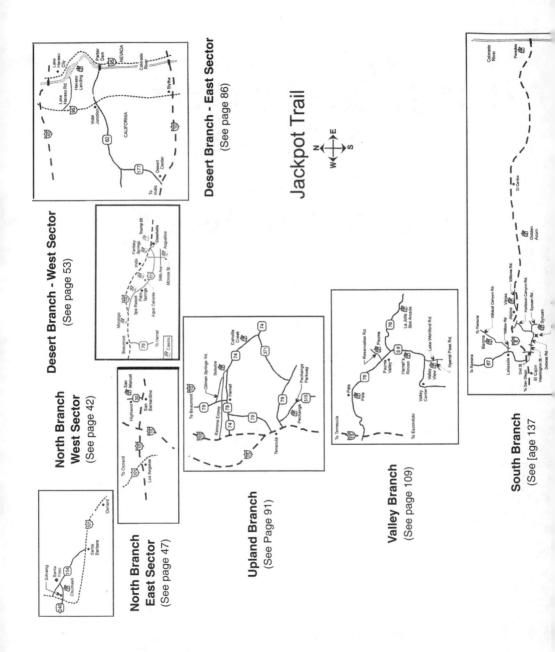

Map 1. Composite — All Branches

JACKPOT TRAIL
INDIAN GAMING
IN SOUTHERN
CALIFORNIA

DAVID J. VALLEY

WITH

DIANA LINDSAY

SUNBELT PUBLICATIONS
SAN DIEGO, CALIFORNIA

Jackpot Trail

Sunbelt Publications
Copyright © David J. Valley, 2003
All rights reserved. First edition 2003
Book design and composition by W. G. Hample & Associates
Edited by Diana Lindsay
Cover design by Handmade Graphics & Computer Concepts
Printed in the United States of America

Sunbelt Publications, Inc.
P.O. Box 191126
San Diego, CA 92159-1126
(619) 258-4911 (619) 258-4916 fax
www.sunbeltpub.com

———————————————————

Library of Congress Cataloging-in-Publication Data

Valley, David J., 1931-
  Jackpot trail : Indian gaming in southern California / David J. Valley
; edited by Diana Lindsay.
      p. cm.
Includes bibliographical references and index.
  ISBN 0-932653-58-8 (pbk. : alk. paper)
  1. Gambling on Indian reservations--California, Southern. 2. Indians
of North America--Gambling--California, Southern. 3.
Casinos--California, Southern. I. Lindsay, Diana, 1944- II. Title.
  E78.C15V13 2003
    795'.09794'9--dc21
                                2002156729

DEDICATION

To generations of Native Americans
who endured untold suffering,
while new Americans
reaped the benefits
of this great land.

END OF THE TRAIL PRAYER

Do not stand at my grave and weep,
I am not there. I do not sleep.
I am a thousand winds that blow,
I am the diamond glint on snow.
I am the sunlight on ripened grain,
I am the gentle autumn rain.

Do not stand at my grave and cry,
I am not there. I did not die.

Author Unknown

CONTENTS

LIST OF MAPS AND CASINO SUMMARIES

PUBLISHER'S FOREWORD

Sunbelt Publications publishes books about "Adventures in Natural and Cultural History." These include natural science and outdoor guidebooks, regional reference, and stories that celebrate the land and its people. Our books, with an underlying theme of "journey," guide readers through time and space and into distinctive communities and special places.

When David Valley first presented his idea for *Jackpot Trail*, it was obvious to me that this could be the format for a unique journey akin to other Sunbelt books. I was personally interested in a book that would be more than just the first-ever guide to the fun and excitement of southern California Indian casinos. I was interested in an approach to this subject that would both educate and enrich the reader's experience beyond the neon and glitz of the casino environment.

My own interest in local Indians stems from my original research into the history of the Anza-Borrego Desert. In both my master's thesis from San Diego State University and in my most recent book, *Anza-Borrego A to Z: People, Places, and Things*, I attempted to present a complete, yet concise, story of the desert Indians. I had hoped someday to extend that interest to include the various bands in San Diego County. Valley's *Jackpot Trail* has even a wider scope and satisfies my original desires and more.

Using casinos as the subject matter, *Jackpot Trail* transports the reader to a much earlier time when each band lived in its own distinct way and later clashed with Anglos, ultimately settling on assigned reservation land that created the environment where future casinos could thrive. On this journey we can come to appreciate what our local Indians have endured. We can celebrate their resilience and ability to create new endeavors that restore pride in their own culture. Indians have contributed to our state's rich history and are now making a distinct economic contribution to its future growth.

It is with pride that we introduce you, our readers, to the unique world of Indian gaming.

Diana Lindsay
Publisher

PREFACE

The idea for this book began with an international telephone call, when my old friend and business associate from Korea, Y. H. Cho, told me of his plans to visit California. Afterwards, thinking of something interesting and different for Mr. Cho to do for a few days while visiting in San Diego, I thought about taking him around to some of the new Indian casinos. I had visited a few, but since I didn't know much about them, I decided to collect some information. I first went to the local Barnes & Noble to pick up a book that I could read and pass on to Mr. Cho. No luck — they had absolutely nothing in stock or on their computer files. The next stop was the library, with the same result — nothing to be found on the subject.

As an engineer and business executive until my retirement, I have always been alert to find unsatisfied needs, for they are the seeds of new enterprise. My guess was the nonexistent book might be a need just waiting for satisfaction. I vetted the idea with my advisory staff, i.e. my wife and sons, and was encouraged by their enthusiasm. Having some experience in writing, with a published nonfiction book under my belt, I felt this opportunity was beckoning to me.[1]

When I had enough of a start on the book to show it to a publisher, I called Sunbelt Publications. I found Sunbelt's name on several attractive guidebooks while doing research in the Barnes & Noble travel section. The people at Sunbelt said they had been expecting an author to bring out a book on the subject of Indian gaming. And, as it turned out, they are eminently suited to publish and distribute this type of book. Lucky me.

The initial concept for the book was for it to be a comprehensive and factual guidebook presenting pertinent information about Indian casinos in southern California. However, with Mr. Cho in mind as a reader, and for others who know little about the Indian background and would like to know more, the concept was expanded to give historic information about the tribes engaged in gaming and to describe the events which led up to the establishment of casinos.

My research into the history of California Indians for background information led to my learning a great deal about the many years of harsh and abusive treatment of Native Americans. So, this book goes well beyond gambling as it tells of the Indian's trials through the past three centuries, up to the present day.

ACKNOWLEDGMENTS

The author wishes to acknowledge and thank the dozens of people associated with Indian gaming in southern California for providing the material and information necessary to prepare this book and encouraging me along the way. I would like to thank some by name, but don't know where to stop. To avoid offending any I may have forgotten to cite, I will take the safer route and offer a general and sincere thank you to all.

I must specifically express my gratitude to my publisher, Sunbelt Publications, and especially mention Diana Lindsay, who serves as president and has been my editor and mentor. Her knowledge of local Indians and her editing skills have been an enormous help to me. And to my dear wife Dottie and family, who always provide the peripheral support and encouragement to keep me going, I am most grateful.

David Valley
January 2003

PHOTO CREDITS

Agua Caliente Casino 67, 68
Anza-Borrego Desert State Park 2, 12, 16, 21
Augustine Casino 72
Barona Valley Ranch Resort and Casino 33, 37, 39, 139, 142, 144
Cahuilla Creek Casino 106
Casino Morongo 56
Casino Pauma 118, 120
Chumash Casino 44
Fantasy Springs Casino 4, 74, 76, 79, 80
Golden Acorn Casino and Travel Center 161
Harrah's Rincon Casino and Resort 127, 129
Havasu Landing Resort and Casino 88, 89

Diana Lindsay 18
Malki Museum 58
Pala Casino 111, 115
Paradise Casino 165
Pechanga Resort and Casino 98, 101, 102
San Manuel Indian Bingo and Casino 49
Soboba Casino 93, 95
Spa Resort Casino 54, 61, 64
Sycuan Casino and Resort 28, 148
Trump 29 Casino 82
David Valley 107, 123, 125
Valley View Casino 133
Viejas Casino and Turf Club xii, 154, 158
Michael Wilken 5

INTRODUCTION

Jackpot Trail is the most complete source of information about the 22 Indian gaming casinos in southern California. This book is not intended to promote gambling but is to be used as an information resource to help those who wish to know more about Indian gaming and what the present-day casinos have to offer in terms of recreation and entertainment. The book covers the history of the tribes now participating in gaming and tells how this new enterprise has affected their livelihood, future, their community, and their neighbors. It is also a trail guide to adventure for exploring some of the more remote areas and backroads of southern California where many of the casinos are found.

At the time of this writing there are 22 active Indian gaming operations in southern California. The latest casino opened in December in Winterhaven. It is an extension of the Paradise Casino in Yuma, Arizona. But that is not all there *will* be. There are also at least four more Indian groups that have been considering casinos. One is the Torres Martinez Band of Desert Cahuilla Indians whose reservation is located in the vicinity of the Salton Sea. Another is the Ewiiaapaayp (pronounced weé-ya-pipe) whose reservation is within a mile of the Viejas Casino. The third is the Manzanita Band of Mission Indians whose reservation is two miles north of the Campo Reservation. The fourth is the Jamul Band of Mission Indians whose reservation is 10 miles east of El Cajon along State Highway 94.

A successful casino has never been handed to Indian tribes on a platter. It has taken many years of hard work and struggle on the part of a tribe or a band to even consider its first gaming enterprise, such as bingo or a card room. It isn't just the work of a few Indians with smart consultants, either. All Indians of a tribe are very much involved, as tribes and bands are organized in a very democratic fashion, whereby each person is party to tribal decisions either directly or through elected members on the tribal council.

Indians take the responsibility of engaging in gaming very seriously. After more than two centuries of being on the short end of the stick, they are cautious and understandably wary, taking nothing for granted. With their new-found success, after taking care of their own needs and those of non-gaming tribes as required by Proposition 5, they are also reaching out to surrounding communities to help others. Hopefully, this book will give readers a better understanding of our Native American neighbors and how Indian gaming can work to everyone's benefit.

Some might say it's a sad commentary on society that gambling and casinos even exist. But whatever the moral issues may be, the practical issue is that people love to gamble for fun and excitement. For southern California Indians, gaming is a respected tradition that predates European contact.

INDIAN GAMING AS A CULTURAL TRADITION

Games were important to the early Indians, as they are now. Some of the more popular games were foot races, hoop games, wrestling, guessing games, games of chance, "dice" games played by women, and team games similar to present-day field hockey. Horse racing also became important after horses were introduced to California. Wagering the most valued possessions on the outcome of a contest was common practice, and those who possessed the skill to win became renowned in their local communities and commanded great respect.

Peon is the best known and most widely played game of chance. It is the Spanish name for a guessing game that calls for great player skill in the art of concealment while controlling facial and bodily expression. Opponents would guess as to the position of concealed playing pieces made from bones (usually made from coyote shin). The bones were on a leather thong that could be slipped around the wrist. Peon has been described as "a game of mental ability, or rather of will and character." Among the Kumeyaay, the game is traditionally played by men, usually at powwows and fiestas when different tribes are present. In some places today, women can play on their own teams. The game can last for several hours. Teams bet before the game begins, but side betting by observers is allowed throughout the game. A large wall mural at the Viejas Casino depicts this ancient traditional game.[2]

Courtesy Viejas Casino and Turf Club

Peon game wall mural at Viejas Casino

Katherine Luomala, writing in the *Handbook of North American Indians*, said, "Betting, instituted by primal twins [the gods of creation], characterized recreation at ceremonies, as in the men's guessing game of peon, the women's stick-dice game, and the hoop and poles, shinny, and other ball games." The custom of gambling was part of the original creation and has always been part of the Indian culture of southern California.[3]

Spaniards first introduced card games to the Indians. One game that is still played is "conquion chiquita" or "old lady's game." Each player was required to put up an ante, and the winner would take the pot.

In 1953, Public Law 280 made it illegal for Indians to play and wager on their traditional games when reservations were made subject to state and county control. Because gambling is prohibited in California, Indians could no longer practice traditional gaming until later legislation allowed it once again on Indian lands.

The reinstitution of gaming on Indian lands follows two centuries of having their lands, rights, and way of life usurped by invasions of white men that left them underemployed, undereducated, undernourished, and without hope for a better life. Unfortunately this is still true for most Indians in the heartland of our country, but where Native Americans have taken the opportunity to develop casinos, such as in southern California, they are now able to confirm their dignity and rebuild Indian communities no longer dependent on government "dole."

RAPID GROWTH OF CASINOS

The Indian gaming business in California, though only in its first decade, is growing rapidly. It is literally changing the landscape in many areas. The extent of its growth and development will likely exceed present expectations.

Indian casinos are being constructed on reservation land that has been considered almost worthless. Land was previously used mostly for grazing and limited farming. Originally, operations were confined to temporary structures or oversized tents, but as the income from gambling revenues multiplied and the operators demonstrated their abilities, the investments grew rapidly for more permanent casinos mimicking those of Las Vegas and Atlantic City, although many on a smaller scale.

California gaming has greater prospects for growth than Las Vegas or any other gaming center for the single and simple reason that it has the largest and most affluent consumer market in the country within its borders. California casinos are within easy reach of millions of Americans. Even though many of the casinos are well off the beaten path, they are many hours nearer than Las Vegas. Also, many southern California casinos now offer superstar entertainment so long associated with Las Vegas.

The dynamics of growth are already taking hold. In the early phase a casino must make enough profit to cover costs and provide a positive cash flow if it is to outgrow temporary quarters and expand. In the next phase profits may grow enough to enable further improvements to the gaming environs by providing more amenities, comfort, posh and pomp. As this pays off by attracting more customers and further increases the cash flow, large-scale investment may finance hotels, golf courses, swimming pools, travel centers, recreational vehicle parks, outlet shopping centers, and other major attractions. For a few casinos this process has already advanced to the later stages. These investments have now reached the multibillion dollar mark and are rising rapidly. *The San Diego Union-Tribune* reported on August 27, 2002, that California is now the second largest "gambling mecca" in the country.[4]

Those who haven't realized the significance of California's Indian casinos should not make the mistake of underestimating their accomplishments compared to their Las Vegas counterparts or the impact they will have on the people and economy of California. Their financial impact in the areas where they are located is quickly felt as millions of dollars of needed goods and services are purchased locally while new jobs are created with the majority of employees being non-Indian.

Here's what the Las Vegas Investment Advisors, Inc. (LVIA), an independent gaming industry research organization, has to say about one of California's most developed casino operation:

> Barona [is] arguably the most advanced slot floor in the world. No doubt, Barona will become something of a "University" for Las Vegas casino executives. It wasn't long ago that Native American casinos had little in the way of financial "horsepower." This is no longer the situation and the business model has now been proven. One frequently hears the views in Las Vegas that the California Native American casinos will never be able to seriously impact southern Nevada's gaming since the latter's destination resorts are the world's best and that California casinos will remain largely day-trip markets. LVIA is not only skeptical of such views but would assert they are pure "Hogwash."[5]

Closer to home, we have observations of the CEO of Venture Catalyst, Don Speer, who has been instrumental in the development of the Barona Casino. The *Barona Casino Journal*, November, 2000, states:

> Speer sees a fierce competition with Nevada casinos in which California casinos will more than hold their own. Within 10 years, California's gaming revenues will be substantially higher than Nevada's.[6]

It was no wonder that Las Vegas gaming interests tried to curtail the growth and development of Indian casinos in California. During elections of the late 1990s when critical legislation was under consideration, Las Vegas groups spent over $100 million to defeat the enabling legislation, but they were stymied by the substantial support of California voters.

Now there are literally billions of dollars financing the Indian gaming industry, some of which is connected to gambling interests that originally tried to keep the lid on the Indian entrepreneurs. Since big names of shrewd operators like Harrah's and Donald Trump are now connected to these enterprises, there's little doubt about their prospects for the future.

In addition, there is room to grow. Much of the Indian land in California is available in relative abundance, compared to the cramped Las Vegas strip, and the year round climate in California is far better. In the next 10 years the gaming resort business will explode. Those now riding the "Jackpot Trail" are modern day pioneers. It won't be too long before readers will be telling others the "I remember when" tales.

TRAVELING THE "JACKPOT TRAIL"

The Jackpot Trail through southern California covers a lot of territory from one end to the other, over 600 miles. It is not a one or two-day outing, by any stretch, but it can be done comfortably over the course of a week if one is well organized, or taken in segments as time allows.

To aid the adventurer who may wish to take on a segment at a time, the *Jackpot Trail* has been broken up into five regional branches with casinos in each branch listed as you might travel to them in sequence from west to east and from north to south. This arrangement is followed in the book to provide continuity and to relate to the special local attractions of each branch. Maps are included for each branch to guide the way. However, for readers who are interested in a particular casino, they may refer to the table of contents or to the list of casino summaries to find the page number of the casino they seek. At the beginning of each casino description there is a single page summary for quick reference.

The North Branch includes only two casinos and covers a wide span of 150 miles between the Chumash Casino in Santa Ynez (Santa Barbara County) and the San Manuel Indian Bingo and Casino in Highland (San Bernardino County).

Moving east, the Desert Branch includes seven casinos, six of which are in relatively close proximity in Riverside County, and the seventh, a 150-mile trip across the desert in San Bernardino County. The Desert Branch casinos are: Casino Morongo in Cabazon, Spa Resort Casino in Palm Springs, Agua Caliente Casino in Rancho Mirage, Fantasy Springs Casino in Indio, Trump 29 Casino and Augustine Casino in Coachella, and the Havasu Landing Resort and Casino at Lake Havasu.

To the south, the Upland Branch includes three casinos in Riverside County: the Cahuilla Creek Casino in Anza, the Soboba Casino in San Jacinto, and the Pechanga Resort and Casino in Temecula.

South of the Upland Branch is the Valley Branch with five casinos in San Diego County: Pala Casino in Pala, the Casino Pauma in Pauma Valley, La Jolla Reservation Slot Arcade also in Pauma Valley, Harrah's Rincon Casino and Resort in Valley Center, and the Valley View Casino also in Valley Center.

Farther south and to the east is the South Branch's five casinos in San Diego and Imperial Counties: Barona Valley Ranch Resort and Casino in Lakeside, Viejas Casino and Turf Club in Alpine, Sycuan Casino and Resort in El Cajon, the Golden Acorn Casino and Travel Center in Campo, and the Paradise Casino in Winterhaven at the Arizona border.

The reader will note as he travels the Jackpot Trail that some casinos are full-fledged resorts while others have limited features that hardly qualify them being called casinos. Regardless of size, however, all have a unique character and attributes that attract customers and keep them coming back. As a first time visitor, keep an open mind. Don't try to compare the smaller casinos to their big brothers, but rather, try to discern their individual nature and understand how they are trying to succeed. You will find that many casinos have passed the point where they are worried about succeeding, while others are still working hard to establish themselves as profitable enterprises.

USING THE BOOK

Overall, the book is organized to provide the reader with ready access to pertinent facts or details for reading the Indians' story at one's leisure. The guidebook portion is found in the second half of the book, starting with the All Casinos Summary Chart on page 40. This chart compares and lists at a glance key information for all 22 casinos, including: location, telephone number, minimum age, size of gaming area, bus service, number of slots and gaming tables, poker room, offtrack betting, bingo, food areas, hotels and special features.

Each casino listing is preceded by an individual summary chart followed by detailed information about tribal history, the casino, games, restaurants, entertainment and other features.

The *Jackpot Trail* is not a book to read and put away. It is suggested that you first read the book through, decide where you wish to start, and bring the book along with you on your travels for handy reference.

Make copies of the log form provided on page xviii for your convenience. The form has an entry for a "starting stake." It's a good idea, especially for novice gamblers, to have a definite stake set aside for gambling and, once that stake is expended, to wager no more on that visit. If you are on a winning streak, who can say what you should do, but it is a good idea to set a "cut-out" limit to keep some winnings once they drop to a certain point. This is what many successful gamblers do to build their bankroll. As the song goes, "you've got to know when to hold 'em and know when to fold 'em." You've also got to learn when to walk away whether as a winner or a loser.

This book is not an aid for experienced gamblers to improve their play; the instructional information about games is rudimentary and intended for the novice. However, it is a handy guide that will acquaint all readers with the full range of choices to help them decide where they wish to visit and play their favorite games.

Once you walk through the casino doors, you are on your own. We hope the *Jackpot Trail* has prepared you to enjoy the experience as much as possible.

FEEDBACK AND MORE

An author always wants to know if he is getting through to his audience, and more specifically, he wants to know what they think of his book. That might be justification enough for an author to seek feedback, but there is greater purpose behind this request.

The *Jackpot Trail* will hopefully encourage readers to participate in the adventure of visiting remote and distant places, to discover what lies beyond the next bend of the road. We would like scouts on the Jackpot Trail to give their impressions of the journey and the casinos, describe interesting features along the way, and share these experiences and their knowledge with others with similar interests.

For those who have Internet access, we invite you to visit the Jackpot Trail website, www.jackpottrail.com, to register and share information. The website will maintain current advisories based on members' input, and from those reports and from other sources, it will present the latest information, including special offers and promotions from casinos.

For those without Internet access, you may write to Jackpot Trail, Post Office Box 501005, San Diego, CA 92150, for information. All who respond will receive a free Jackpot Trail window decal.

JACKPOT TRAIL DECAL

LOG FORM

Persons

_____

_____

Time

Start_____ : _____   a.m. p.m.

End _____ : _____   a.m. p.m.

Elapsed Hrs.____Mins____

Departing From

_____

Date

_____

Mileage

End

Start

Elapsed Miles _____

Stake

Start $

End $

Net $

Souvenirs

Club   Poker
Card   Chip

Rate quality 0 to 5 ☆ (best)   Rate prices low = L$, moderate = M$, high = H$

Casinos

Layout ____ ☆   Hospitality ____ ☆

Slots ____ ☆   Appearance ____ ☆

Videos ____ ☆   Air Quality ____ ☆

Tables ____ ☆   Restrooms ____ ☆

Restaurants

Buffet ____ ☆ ____ $

Full Service ____ ☆ ____ $

Snack Bar ____ ☆ ____ $

Other ____ ☆ ____ $

OVERALL RATING   ☆

Comments & Notes

_____

_____

_____

_____

PART ONE — HISTORY AND EVOLUTION

CHAPTER 1
INDIANS OF SOUTHERN CALIFORNIA

According to archaeologists, Indians are thought to have lived in southern California beginning 10,000 to 20,000 years ago, but according to their own oral traditions, the Indians have always been here. Even in the last millennium, the period of their history that is known best, tribal identification and territorial limits are uncertain. The lack of any written history until late in the 18th Century is one reason. Another reason, from what can be gleaned from archaeological evidence and traditional oral histories, is that Indian tribes and bands often moved from place to place, other groups migrated into the same areas, and there was assimilation or integration of different groups. Further complications arose from the loss of group or clan names to identify a group of Indians over long periods of time.

The best evidence of tribal histories and place origins has been developed by ethnologists who have established locales and time lines, based on studies of present-day Indian languages and dialects. The location of today's reservations does not often reflect where those bands originally lived for hundreds, or even thousands of years prior to contact.

For these early Indians, southern California was an ideal place. They dwelled in a temperate zone where minimal clothing sufficed. Their daily sustenance was derived from wild game, fish, native fruits, nuts and grains. Fresh water, while not overly abundant, was generally adequate and pure.

This is not to say that Indians had all their needs satisfied with little or no effort. They had to plant, manage those native plants, harvest, hunt, and fish for food. They had to construct protection against the elements, deal with fires, droughts, and other natural disasters.

A key to survival for California's gathering and milling societies was the ability to make storage and cooking containers. This was of major importance in the evolution of all peoples. Many Native Americans made vessels first from animal skins and woven baskets and later from pottery. The methods of individual tribes and bands were distinctive and reflected the availability of materials and the technology of the time.

Most of their sustenance came from the soil and was supplemented with meat from small game. They assiduously harvested small grains by brushing grasses and bushes with finely woven collection baskets, mostly a chore for the

Courtesy Anza-Borrego Desert State Park

Cooking gathered foods in baskets

women and children. These grains were ground into a flour using stone mortars and pestles to make a simple bread staple.

Food was cooked in tightly woven baskets or pottery by immersing thoroughly heated stones into the vessels containing water and food items. The heated stones boiled water and sustained heating for an adequate time to cook small game, vegetables, or a mush of ground nuts and grains.

In the southern California lowlands, living quarters were fashioned from readily available materials. Small limbs and brush were used for structures. Weatherproof thatches were made of grasses and reeds. During warm weather, men and children wore little or no clothing while women typically wore skirts of grass or beaten bark. During cooler weather, simple outer garments were worn, such as rabbit skin blankets. They mostly went barefoot. For traveling on rough terrain, they fashioned sandals of fibrous material.

Pollution as we know it today was unknown — mainly because of the low density of population in a vast territory. Even in more populated areas, the Indian impact on the environment was minimal and mitigated by their ingenuity and instincts. They employed methods for conservation of water, selective cultivation, and crop rotation. They regularly burned valleys, and their burning schedule depended on the use of the land. In essence, they managed the land. It was not until the advent of the white man, who introduced grazing animals and poor agricultural practices, that much of southern California reverted to wilderness and desert wasteland.[7]

Before the coming of the white man, Indians were subject to occasional conflicts with neighboring tribes or even among members within their own tribe, which were sometimes fought with enough intensity that combatants were killed. But these were usually of short duration. Conflicts that did arise might have been triggered by territorial disputes or the unauthorized taking of prospective brides.

All Indian groups in southern California regularly traded with their neighbors, both far and near. Numerous trade trails crossed the area. One major trail connecting the coast to the desert is today's Interstate 8. Indians of the San Diego area traded with the Chumash of Santa Barbara and the Indians of Baja California. Trade items included food, baskets, pottery, and other manufactured items such as jewelry — necklaces, hair ornaments, and pendants made from shells, bone, or stone.

Social customs varied from tribe to tribe, but the majority of southern California tribes were patrilineal with the children tracing their lineage through their father. Children learned by observation. Puberty was marked by initiation ceremonies and learning all that was needed to be an adult. Women's chins were generally tattooed as part of the puberty ceremony. This denoted their clan or family affiliation. Women were respected but not equal to men.

California Indians were highly civilized within the context of their society. They were very strictly organized, and there were societal expectations and taboos that regulated individual expression. They followed accepted practices of behavior and rarely were there serious disputes within a tribe or band. Serious misbehavior was simply not tolerated. They had no need to maintain armed peacekeepers or prisons. Since survival depended on group cooperation, the threat of death or expulsion from the group was the greatest deterrent from aggressive or violent action within the group.

Indian government was organized very differently than the state and European governments. They were organized into semi-autonomous family bands. A band leader was the headman of an extended family or clan. He could make suggestions to a group, but he was not allowed to impose his own power or opinions on the group. At one time there may have been as many as 20 to 30 different bands in San Diego alone, each with its own leader.

Nor were they lacking in religion or spirituality. They believed the spirit continued to exist after death, and they were receptive to supernatural effects at birth, puberty, and death. They participated in extensive religious practices, usually under the direction of a specially endowed priest known as a shaman. Chants, dancing, and body painting were used in religious practices.

Tribal history was recorded through an oral tradition by way of songs. Those who sang the songs were known as "bird singers." Songs were also used for entertainment, for prayers, and for story telling. Songs were often accompanied by instruments, such as gourd rattles, flutes, or whistles. Rhythmic

Courtesy Fantasy Springs Casino

A modern-day dancer at a powwow at Cabazon

dancing was an expressive accompaniment to songs. Rock art, painted or etched art on rock surfaces, was also important for both conveying information and for ceremonial purposes. Forms could be abstract or symbolic.[8]

The well-established cultural and social traditions found in southern California began to unravel in the late 1700s when the first Spaniards arrived in California.

COMING OF THE WHITE MAN

When missions were established in California, their leaders imposed order on the free ranging Indians. Despite the good will of some of the clergy, the missions systematically destroyed the Indian way of life, turning their indigenous collection areas into grazing pasture for sheep and cattle, cutting them off from ocean fishing and hunting areas by restricting their labor to the missions, and eventually breaking their links to the past so thoroughly that the Indians became totally dependent on the missions. The Indian way of life was totally disrupted and nearly extinguished. Under the mission system, the Indians' existence was nothing less than forced bondage. They were, for all practical considerations, slaves. It is documented that any that tried to escape were brought back in chains and beaten, or shot and killed. Even their identity was taken away.

Indian tribes were named after the missions that dominated their lives. For example, the first mission, San Diego de Alcalá, founded in 1769, gave rise to the use of the term Diegueño for the local Yuman speaking tribes, whereas the local Yuman speaking tribes are known today as the Kumeyaay, which is derived from territorial dialect differences. They are also known by the dialects they speak, which include Ipai (some bands spell it Ipay or 'Iipay) and Tipai (or Tipay). The Luiseño tribal name was derived from the San Luis Rey Mission (Washxayam people), the Juaneño from the San Juan Capistrano Mission (Ajachemem people), and the Gabrielino from the San Gabriel Arcángel Mission in Los Angeles (Tongva people). The suffix "eño" means "people of." Hence the Indians were known as people of a particular mission. Adding more confusion to identity, many tribes were simply called "Mission Indians," which has become a nonspecific generic name. Indians' individual names were also abandoned and they were given, or adopted, Spanish names as they were missionized.

Missionization of the Indians had a devastating impact. Foreigners tried to wipe out the Indian's culture, language and way of life. They nearly succeeded with this "culturecide" and certainly decimated the population through the rampant spread of diseases, such as smallpox and measles.

Photo by Michael Wilken

Pottery making — the finishing touches

For an accurate historical perspective of the fate of the southern California Indian bands, the account written by Father William Hughes and published in the *Indian Sentinel* in 1910 is both shocking and disturbing:

Of the thirty thousand Indians at one time attached to the missions, and uncounted thousands in the hills never converted, the official census shows less than three thousand of their descendants in southern California today [1910].

Among the old missions, a few only have any Indians in attendance at all. San Diego, the first mission to be established, which, at the zenith of its glory, in 1800, numbered over fifteen hundred, now has less than fifteen souls. San Luis Rey, which in 1810 had a thousand neophytes, musters now only as many as can be counted on the fingers of two hands. At San Juan Capistrano, in 1812 there were nearly fourteen hundred souls; today there are not more than five families.... Of the *asistencias*, or chapels, original offshoots of the main missions, San Antonio de Pala has about 250 Indians; though few are children of the original inhabitants. For the rest, remnants are found in the mountains above Warner's Ranch [Los Coyotes Indian Reservation], around San Jacinto, or on the desert below Banning. A poor torn band of forty are huddled together on the San Manuel Reservation near San Bernardino [Highland], which comprises six hundred and forty acres, which is described in a calm, judicial government report as "worthless dry hills," and which constitutes all that remains of the once happy outmission of San Gabriel.

Driven from the fertile valley of San Felipe, above which their deserted homes and chapel now hide themselves in sorrow among the ancient oaks; evicted from the great plain of Warner's Ranch and the almost sacred Agua Caliente, in order to be transported to black Pala; forced, by encroachments of white men even upon the desert, to find refuge in cold Cahuilla, and pressed back by degrees from the mesa of San Jacinto til [sic] they have taken up their last stand on the sand dunes of Soboba; is it any wonder that they are a sad and demoralized race?[9]

What a scathing indictment of the mission system and the intrusion of white men on the lives of Indians of southern California written by a "man of the cloth."

The map which follows shows the rough outlines of major tribal areas, mission names and locations, and the most closely associated cities of the present day. Within each tribal area there were many independent villages named for the bands of Indians that established them. The only band names shown on the

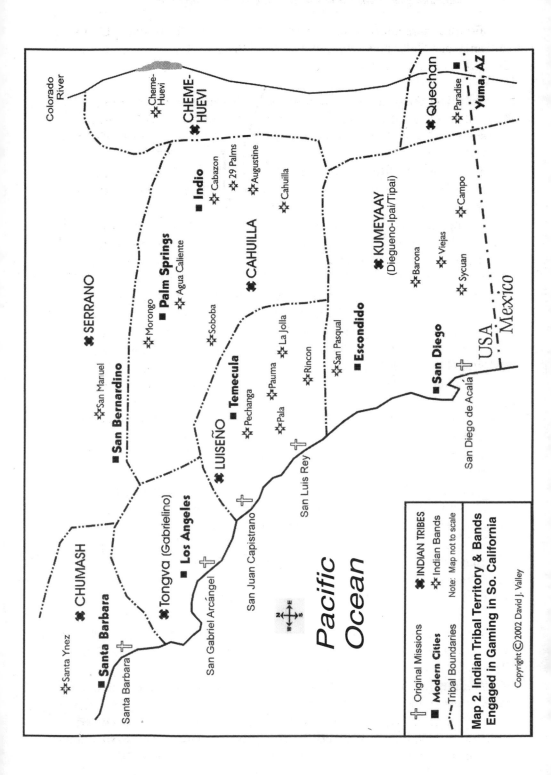

Map 2. Indian Tribal Territory & Bands
Engaged in Gaming in So. California

Original Missions	✳ INDIAN TRIBES
■ Modern Cities	✳ Indian Bands
Tribal Boundaries	Note: Map not to scale

Copyright © 2002 David J. Valley

CHUMASH
✳ Santa Ynez
✳ Santa Barbara
■ Santa Barbara
Santa Barbara

Tongva (Gabrielino)
■ Los Angeles
San Gabriel Arcángel
San Juan Capistrano

SERRANO
✳ San Manuel
■ San Bernardino
✳ Morongo

LUISEÑO
■ Temecula
✳ Pechanga
✳ Pala
✳ Pauma
✳ La Jolla
✳ Rincon
San Luis Rey
✳ Soboba

Palm Springs
■ Palm Springs
✳ Agua Caliente

Indio
■ Indio
✳ Cabazon
✳ 29 Palms
✳ Augustine
✳ Cahuilla

CAHUILLA

CHEME-HUEVI
✳ Cheme-Huevi
✳ CHEME-HUEVI
Colorado River

Quechan
✳ Quechan
■ Paradise
Yuma, AZ

KUMEYAAY
(Diegueno-Ipai/Tipai)
✳ Barona
✳ Viejas
✳ Sycuan
✳ Campo

Escondido
■ Escondido
✳ San Pasqual

San Diego
■ San Diego
San Diego de Acalá

USA
Mexico

Pacific Ocean

N
W - E
S

map are those currently associated with casinos. There were as many as 50 bands in some of the tribal areas and many of these exist today.

CHANGES BRING NO IMPROVEMENTS

The Mexican government secularized the missions in 1834, undoing the Roman Catholic Church's control over the Indians. Not long afterward, California was ceded by Mexico to the United States, setting the Indians up for a new version of oppression and control. The mid-1800s brought about the discovery of gold in California and a great migration of Anglo-Americans. The upshot of all of this for the Indians was a change from one type of bondage to another. Early settlers considered the prior bondage and servitude to missions as evidence that the Indians had no indigenous rights. Over this period a small number of Indians did manage to establish freehold properties and received allotments of properties by the government, but most were subject to outright taking of their lands by the powerful. If Indian land was attractive, for agricultural or other use, it was often confiscated by one means or another. If the land was too poor to be attractive, the Indians were permitted to hold it, though they could barely survive on its meager yield.

THE "EIGHTEENS" SCAM

One of the earliest and most significant actions by the federal government, ostensibly to protect Indian land rights, whether intentioned or not, turned out to be the biggest land scam in history. It is called the Eighteen Treaties of the early 1850s after the eighteen bands of Indians that government representatives met with in northern California. These bands were selected more on the basis of convenience than for having any authority to speak for all the Indians in California. Nevertheless, an agreement was prepared by government agents, which stipulated that Indians of California would be granted permanent and exclusive rights to about 20 distinct areas in the state, from the northernmost to southernmost borders.

On good faith, many Indians gave up other land holdings and moved to the appointed areas. For more than 50 years, Indians were not told that this so-called treaty had no force of law as it was never ratified by the U.S. Senate. The door was open for takeover of most of the Indian lands in the state.

The downward spiraling of Indians' property rights was abated in the late 1800s as Congress and executive orders established new reservations. This was not necessarily a great boon to the Indians, as reservations were usually established in areas of marginal land quality, but it drew a line in the sand that to some extent prevented complete takeover of their lands.

According to the Eighteen Treaties, a total of 7.5 million acres was set aside for the Indians out of the more than 100 million acres in California. What the Indians eventually managed to keep was only half a million acres. Indians became wards of the U.S. government and were managed for decades by the Bureau of Indian Affairs (BIA), which has an abysmal record of failing to deal fairly or effectively with their charges.

THE GREAT IRONY

The desire to take land of any value away from the Indians was actually part of a greater global quest for worldwide discovery and dominance, from about 1450 to 1850, primarily by rulers of European civilization. Advancements in technology beginning in 1450, specifically the ability to build sea-going vessels that could traverse global distances, along with the skill to navigate to and from distant points, made this possible.

Wealthy and powerful rulers of European nations, chiefly Portugal and Spain, seized on the opportunities to increase their wealth by discovering (more accurately, finding and colonizing for plunder and exploitation) far off lands. Kings and queens commissioned merchants and outfitted great ships with military forces and administrators to do their bidding. Also there was, as a silent partner, the Catholic Church of Rome, with their spiritual and secular agendas. To be fair, many of the religious leaders and most of the lower-level clerics were spiritually motivated men of God, but the church's motivation was tainted by the passion for wealth and power.

This lust for wealth brought the first white man, Juan Rodríguez Cabrillo, a Portuguese mariner who sailed for the king of Spain, to the shores of California in the year 1542. Two centuries later, in 1769, Indians felt the full force of European passions when the Spaniards returned and the first mission was established at what became San Diego in the Spanish territory of California. Missionization of the Indians followed until the mid-1800s, when the missions were secularized and broken up by the succeeding Mexican government. Anglo-Americans followed with their quest for gold and land.

Now, hundreds of years after the global quest began, Indians are using the white man's quest for wealth and pleasure to their own advantage. With Indian gaming generating large revenues for many Indian tribes, their future independence and prosperity is assured.

GENERAL TRIBAL HISTORIES

CHUMASH

The Chumash (pronounced 'shoo-mash), who now have a casino on the Santa Ynez Reservation near Solvang in Santa Barbara County, originally ranged over a vast territory from Monterey all the way south to Malibu, a territory that incorporated the original missions of San Luis Obispo and Santa Barbara.

The Chumash tribe was at one time the largest tribe in California, numbering well over 10,000 members at the time of the first missions. By 1886, however, fewer than 100 Indians could be located, and these numbers dropped by the turn of the century. The Chumash language is classified Hokan, which, as a language stock, is probably the oldest in California and is linguistically related to the Kumeyaay. However, their spoken language is almost extinct. The last person known to speak the Chumash language died in 1982.

Starting in 1772 the Spaniards built five missions in Chumash territory. The last one was built at Santa Ynez and was founded in 1804 by Fr. Estebán Tapis. Santa Ynez is named after Saint Agnes, a 13-year-old girl martyred in the 4th Century in Rome. She is the patron saint of chastity. Father Tapis was a faithful man of God who diligently cared for his flock and taught Indian boys to read and write. He was loved and admired for his piety and devotion to his followers.

Of the California coastal Indians, the Chumash were by far the best seamen. From early times they devised a way of making oceangoing canoe-like crafts of wooden planks, rather than the hollowed out logs or birch-bark canoes made by other Indians. Fastening the planks together to make them both sturdy and waterproof without nails or other fasteners demonstrated their ingenuity (Just hewing planks with stone tools was quite a feat in itself.). Finished planks were drilled in many places along the joining edges and bound together with strong cords made from fibrous plant strings and animal sinew. A resinous tar substance, which bubbled up from the ground, was applied to the joints to make them waterproof.[10] The resulting craft was rather boxy, with sloping bow and stern, but seaworthy enough to make trips of 40 miles or more to neighboring islands where many of the Chumash permanently settled. The place where the Chumash were known to make their trademark vessels was later named Carpinteria.

The Chumash were clever in other ways, too. They fashioned cooking pots and bowls from the mineral steatite or soapstone, which was mined on Santa Catalina Island. Steatite can be heated in open fires without breaking. The stone can be readily fashioned with a sharp edged stone or knife, as it is relatively soft. However the ingredient in steatite that gives it good thermal properties is asbestos, and those that worked with it extensively may have been early cancer victims.

The Chumash had interesting social customs and ceremonies, the most unusual of which was male-female (couples) dancing, which was done to music provided by flutes, whistles, rattles, and singing. No heavy percussion instruments, such as drums, were used. The Chumash were avid gamblers.[11]

SERRANO

The Serrano Indians lived in the San Bernardino Mountains and nearby Mojave Desert for centuries, perhaps as long as 1,000 to 2,500 years before the coming of the white man. Their language indicates they belong to the Takic branch of the Uto-Aztecan language family, related to Cahuilla, Cupeño, Luiseño, and Gabrielino or Tongva. Of known Indian tribes of long standing, they were probably related to the Ute tribe or Paiute tribe.

The name Serrano, meaning mountaineer or highlander, was given to the indigenous people of the region by the Spaniards after they established Mission San Gabriel Arcángel in 1771 in the vicinity of present-day Los Angeles. Apparently the name of the adjacent community Highland originated from the same source. The Serrano, however, call themselves Takhtam. Their territory included much of San Bernardino and Riverside counties and as far south as Temecula. Their territory was rich with game, fresh water, and edible plants, and the climate at lower elevations was moderate year round, all of which provided a very desirable place to live. Their population was probably no higher than 1,500 at any time, a low density, which did not over tax their relatively large territory.

The Serrano occupied many villages, each with a population of 100-150 persons. A village had two distinct lineages known as moieties, the *Wildcats* and the *Coyotes*. Persons within the same moiety could not marry one another. A spouse had to come from the other moiety group. This practice helped to reduce close inbreeding of their small communities.

The story of the Serrano tribe's tribulations and struggle for survival after the coming of the white man is similar to that of other California Indians, although missionization wasn't a big influence until 1819 when an asistencia was created in Redlands.

The Serrano reservation was established in 1891 as the San Manuel Reservation, named after their great tribal leader, Santos Manuel. The federal government established the reservation trust on 740 acres of land in the foothills of the San Bernardino Mountains, to the north of the city of Highland. The land, because of its slopes, was not well suited for farming, and those who remained on the reservation lived in crude adobe huts without running water or electricity in a state of poverty until about the middle of the 20th Century.

Although the population was reduced to a mere 100 by 1900, the 2000 census listed about 150 Serranos, according to the Native American Historical Data Base (NAHDB).[12] Of this number, about half live on the reservation today.

The San Manuel Indians now have a more diverse heritage because Serranos have married those of Cahuilla, Kumeyaay, Paiute, and other Indian and non-Indian origins. Those who have reached the legal age (21) are voting members of the tribal general council and exercise democratic voting rights on all decisions affecting the band.

CAHUILLA

The Cahuilla tribe (pronounced cah-wee´-yah) inhabited over 2,400 square miles of the arid inland regions and mountain ranges of southern California. They lived from the San Bernardino Mountains, through Palm Springs and the Coachella Valley area to the Anza-Borrego Desert and from Idyllwild to Anza. Archaeologists say they came to this area from the north about 1,500 to 2,000 years ago (and possibly as much as 4,000 years ago), although their own oral tradition states that they were created here. Because of the vastness of the territory and its limited resources of food and game, the Cahuilla developed into many distinct and independent bands. Their language is part of the Uto-Aztecan family and is related to the Serrano, Luiseño, and Cupeño.

Amount and timing of rainfall were crucial to these Indians. In times of drought as wells dried up, large migrations were made to areas where mountain streams or springs could be found. An overabundance of rain at the wrong time could also be a problem. During the harvesting of acorns, a major food staple, heavy rainfall could destroy much of the crop. A specially endowed Indian shaman, who traveled from village to village, conducted rain ceremonies to help manage this critical natural element.

For hundreds of years many lived around the now extinct Lake Cahuilla in the vicinity of the present-day Salton Sea. These Indians enjoyed fish and shellfish from the lake and took advantage of the small game the lake attracted. The lake dried up about 1500, after which these groups moved closer to the mountains and reverted to more of the grain, mesquite, and acorn diet.

Courtesy Anza-Borrego Desert State Park

Cahuilla basketry

The mountains in this region range up to 9,000 feet in elevation. The lower elevations, around 3,500 feet, and the canyons leading into the desert provided a greater variety of plant life and game, as well as water resources. During summer the Cahuilla lived in the canyons and harvested mesquite on the desert floor. In fall they moved to higher elevations to harvest acorns and pinyon nuts, and in winter and spring they harvested desert agave and other plants. Larger game such as deer, mountain sheep, and antelope were found at about the 3,500-foot elevation. The Cahuilla were very well adapted to the wide range of living conditions of the southern California desert and surrounding mountains.

Because of their remoteness, they had less contact with the missions and white men than other southern California Indians, but even so, they were struck by the smallpox epidemic of 1883, which reduced their numbers from about 3,000 to 1,000. However, because of their many bands and diversity of locations, a larger percentage of their members survived than other stricken tribes.

Generally, warfare was a last resort, but it was known, as recorded through war songs and the presence of weapons. It is known that they fought the Mohave who were often aggressors. They also fought the Luiseño in 1847 when the Luiseño, who occupied territory to the south and west of the Cahuilla, sided with Americans to fight against the Mexican-Californians. The Cahuilla were greatly offended by the Luiseño alliance. Members of the two tribes met in battle at Aguanga, where the Cahuilla overwhelmed the Luiseño. This historic event is known as the Aguanga Massacre.

In the late 1800s Americans developed large cattle ranches on what were formerly Cahuilla lands, employing many of the Indians as ranch hands. The Indians became excellent range hands. Some Indians with land of their own used their skills to become ranchers themselves, but they never had the economic resources to engage in large scale ranching. In any case, it is likely that an Indian enterprise considered to be valuable by the white men would have been confiscated.

Within the old Cahuilla territory there are currently eight casinos, going from west to east and north to south they are: Morongo, Spa Resort, Agua Caliente, Fantasy Springs, Trump 29, Augustine, Soboba, and Cahuilla Creek. For more information about their individual tribal and band histories, see "Tribal History" in each casino's description.

CHEMEHUEVI

The Chemehuevi (pronounced ché-me-way-vy) Indians are relative newcomers to southern California, having first migrated here about 1700 from Nevada, Utah and Arizona. They were a nomadic tribe whose origins trace back to Ute and southern Paiute Indians and, according to ethnologists, the tribes share a common language called southern Numic. This language is distinctly different from the language of the Mohave Indians, who were their neighbors and earlier occupants of the area known now as the Mojave Desert.

The Chemehuevi, although located mostly on the western side of the Colorado River, traveled over much of the Mojave Desert and up into the foothills of the San Bernardino Mountains. Since the land they occupied provided little sustenance, they moved frequently, sometimes on a seasonal basis, or in response to unusual weather conditions. In the fall they went to the mountains to harvest pinyon nuts, which provided a staple for winter months, supplementing their diet of small game, reptiles, and desert plants.

According to historians, the Chemehuevi were not aggressive. In fact they were known as the "timid" tribe. Their migrations sometimes placed them in the vicinity of Mohave Indians and resulted in skirmishes, for which the more aggressive Mohave were better suited. They fled from their own territories and went to the Cahuilla for refuge and for aid in fighting the Mohave. Over the years, even before the problems resulting from the intrusion of the white man, this tribal warfare took its toll on the Chemehuevi.

Like other tribes, they had no written language, but they created many petroglyphs which can be found throughout the vast Mojave Desert area they traveled. Their traditions, culture, and everyday information, such as location of water, game trails, directions for travel, etc., were maintained and conveyed by way of songs. Certain songs were the property of the family or social group that created them and were carefully passed on to successive generations to contribute to their future welfare. It is an interesting thought that the Chemehuevi Indians recognized intellectual property rights.

The Chemehuevi could have competed with athletes of today, as they were known to be great runners for distance as well as for speed and agility. They were capable of chasing game until the animal tired and could be caught. They may have made good pitchers too, as one of their common hunting weapons was a stone that they could hurl with great accuracy to bring down small game.

The Chemehuevi had many shamans who were specialists — hunting shamans, shamans who found water, and shamans who could bring on or stop rain. The most powerful shamans, called *powands*, used plants for meditation and divined messages by interpreting dreams. They had the power to cure illness and dispel evil spirits.

There is conflicting information about the size of the Chemehuevi tribe. Some indicate the tribe never had more than 800 to 1,000 members. According to the Four Directions Institute, their number was about 1,000 in 1700, up to 1,550 in 1770 (estimate of noted anthropologist Alfred L. Kroeber), dropping to 300 in 1910 (Kroeber estimate), and as low as 36 in 1973, (BIA estimate).[13] An increase was later cited for the year 2000, to 150 (NAHDB estimate). The present estimate of tribal membership is about 700, of which about one-quarter live on the reservation. The recent increase in tribal membership is probably due to the tribe's relaxed criteria for granting membership based on a relatively low percentage of tribal ancestry.

Land claims of the Chemehuevi tribe have been disputed over the past 100 years or more, although the current reservation containing 30,654 acres is a securely established land trust. It has been reported that the Chemehuevi sold tribal land located on the west bank of the Colorado River on two occasions. The construction of the Parker Dam, which created Lake Havasu, was also responsible for much of the controversy.

In 1951 the Chemehuevi petitioned for recognition of their ownership of over 3.6 million acres, an amount equal to half of the most generous offer government agents made for all California Indians (see the "Eighteens" Scam). They eventually settled for about one percent of their claim. The uneven handling of land issues by the government also created problems for white settlers who thought they were occupying authorized areas, some of which were under government land leases. Later the government ceded some of the same land back to the Chemehuevi, thereby putting white occupants under Indian control. Disputes over such matters are still going on.

The Havasu Landing Resort and Casino on the Colorado River is owned by the Chemehuevi tribe. The Twentynine Palms Band of Mission Indians, which owns the Trump 29 Casino much farther to the west in Coachella, are also Chemehuevi.

LUISEÑO

The Luiseño (pronounced loowi-sane-yo) tribe occupied territory south of the Gabrielino (Tongva), going east to present-day Temecula and south to the northern border of San Diego County. The division between the Ipai (Ipay or 'Iipay) and Luiseño is the San Luis Rey River. Though a much smaller territory than that occupied by the Cahuilla, the Luiseño territory had more abundant food and game and supported a larger population, which has been estimated to be between 5,000 and 10,000 people prior to Spanish contact. Their diet was more diverse and richer in protein than that of inland Indians. These people were spread throughout the region in as many as 50 separate villages. They were considered to be dangerous and warlike by their neighbors. They had elaborate war leadership structures. They were also known as an agricultural and artisan group.

There were two missions in the Luiseño territory, San Juan Capistrano, founded in 1775, and San Luis Rey, built 23 years later in 1798. It was after the San Luis Rey Mission that the identifying name of Luiseño was coined. Whatever tribal name was used prior to 1800 is not clear from historical accounts, although the Luiseño of Rincon call themselves Washxayam.

Dolan H. Eargle Jr. in his book, *Native California Guide*, writes, "For some reason the padres allowed the Luiseño to live normal lives in their villages."[14] This was the policy at San Luis Rey. The padres at San Juan Capistrano Mission, on the other hand, forced the Indians to live at the mission. This was more the norm, as it is known that the history of the missions was fraught with conflicts between the local Indians, particularly with the Luiseño and whites. The conversion and reculturization of Indians by the missions was of little or no advantage, but the damage inflicted was monumental.

Five reservations were eventually established in the Luiseño territory. They include Pala, Rincon, La Jolla, Pauma-Yuima, and Pechanga. Soboba was established as a Cahuilla reservation but is today a Luiseño reservation. All now have casinos. The San Luis Rey Band of Mission Indians, which is associated with the original mission, was never placed on a separate reservation. They are the only Luiseño band not to have a casino now. The center for this band's activities is the mission.

KUMEYAAY

South of the Luiseño and Cahuilla tribes were the Kumeyaay (pronounced ku-may´-yai), who are also known by the mission name of Diegueño and by older Indian tribal names of Tipai (Tipay), in the south, and Ipai (Ipay or 'Ii-pay), in the north. They lived in San Diego County, bounded by the ocean on the west and Imperial County on the east, and extending as far to the south as Ensenada in Baja California, Mexico. Their native language comes from the Yuman branch of the Hokan family and is related to the Chumash and Quechan.

The coastal Kumeyaay kept more to the inland hills and plains, subsisting more on wild fruit, grains, and nuts. They fished in the ocean and in sloughs for

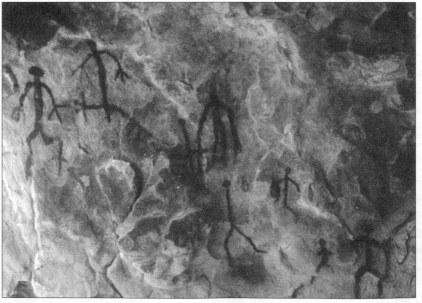

Courtesy Anza-Borrego Desert State Park

Kumeyaay rock art

clams and mussels. Abalone was a favorite. Fish bones and shells have been found in the San Diego mountains.

They also cultivated land and planted crops. Kumeyaay men hunted game, ranging from small game and birds to the larger hoofed animals such as antelope and deer. Legends indicate they understood astronomy and used their knowledge of the heavens to plan their seasonal activities such as planting and harvest.

Men crafted fishhooks, arrows, bows, axes, nets and other implements. Kumeyaay women made finely woven baskets, pottery, clothing, and were the primary builders of housing shelters, which varied with the seasons and the tribes locale. The Kumeyaay practiced animal husbandry and individual family land ownership. Land parcels were passed on through family and clan inheritance. Some agricultural plots were distant from the family's abode and cultivated on a seasonal basis.

Jessica Maxwell in the May-June 1995 issue of *Audubon Magazine* adds an interesting commentary to the above observations:

> When the Spanish first saw the meadows of the mountain valleys east of what we now call San Diego, they pronounced them "excellent pasture." They assumed them to be natural and, being European herdsmen, considered them prime grazing land. The early invaders were, in fact, gazing upon the ancient grain fields of the indigenous Kumeyaay Indians, some of the earliest — and best — environmental managers in North America.[15]

Beginning in 1769, the Kumeyaay were the first Native Americans to experience missionization and did not readily take to the entreaties of the missionaries. They were wooed and plied with gifts, which they readily accepted, and they apparently helped themselves to whatever else they could lay their hands on, according to some accounts. Kumeyaay were openly unfriendly toward the missionaries, suspecting the foreigners were not to be trusted. The first year of the mission, there was only a handful of converts.

Father Junípero Serra, the founder of the California mission system, moved the San Diego Mission away from the military garrison at the Presidio. He wanted to separate the Indians from the soldiers who were a threat to the women. He also wanted to be nearer to the Indians' settlement. A larger mission was built about three miles to the east. However, this move seemed to have an effect opposite than was intended. The night of November 4, 1775, the new mission was surrounded by about 1,000 hostile Indians and attacked. They looted the buildings and set them afire. Several occupants were killed trying to escape, among them Father Luís Jayme, whose body was mutilated.

The uprising was in part a revolt against Spanish men and soldiers who were abusing and raping Indian women. Some women had been forcibly taken in raids, while other Indian women were fooled into believing the Spaniards were interested in marriage.

This deadly raid may have vented some of the Indians' anger, and there followed a peaceful period, although without full acquiescence to the white men. Many Indians helped with the rebuilding of the mission, and gradually more and more Indians accepted conversion to Christianity and mission rule. The exceptions were Kumeyaay who lived to the east of the mission and managed to escape much of the disease and hardship suffered by those who lived near the mission.

When the mission system was discontinued in 1834, by order of the Mexican government, many Indians did not have any alternate opportunities and were thrust into abject poverty. In time some were assimilated into mainstream society, while others sought out Indians who were still able to live off the land in remote areas and joined them. The few who had been trained at the mission as blacksmiths, boot makers, masons, bakers, and in other skills became a resourceful workforce for the growing community of San Diego.

The East County Kumeyaay were again the exceptions who resisted Mexican rule and waged war on Mexican ranchos. The early Californians were on constant alert for Indian attacks.

In 1846 during the Mexican War, General Stephen Watts Kearny brought U.S. troops into Kumeyaay lands and negotiated a "live and let live" policy for the Kumeyaay to stay out of the fight with the Mexicans. At the termination of

Photo by Diana Lindsay

Kumeyaay pottery ready to be fired

the war, the new U.S. border was drawn through the middle of Kumeyaay lands (which extended down to Ensenada, Mexico), and a treaty was signed at Santa Ysabel. Like many other so-called treaties that Indians entered into in good faith, this treaty was never ratified and soon the exploitation of Indian lands began anew. The land grab was finally brought to some order in 1875, when executive orders mandated the formation of Indian reservations. Today there are 13 bands and reservations for the Kumeyaay of San Diego County.

Many Kumeyaay traditions have been passed down through generations and are maintained to the present day. Tribal members gather in times of celebration and grief, on occasions ranging from weddings to deaths to sing, dance, and share the company of friends. At the heart of modern-day Kumeyaay culture are "bird songs," the last of an allegorical cycle of approximately 300 pieces passed down through generations and kept alive by the Kumeyaay bird singers. In place of a written language, the ancient songs serve to perpetuate the lifestyle and philosophy of the Kumeyaay. Singers have found lasting satisfaction and purpose through perpetuating and sharing their people's history and culture through bird songs.

The modern roles of Kumeyaay men and women reflect those of society at large. Traditionally, women have held an equal voice in tribal decisions and government. In common with the larger culture, the Kumeyaay value freedom of religion and expression, the right of self-determination, the opportunity to live in peace, adequate housing, education for the children, and the maintenance of a healthy and safe environment free from crime and pollution.

QUECHAN

In earlier times, the Quechan (pronounced kwa-tsan) were known as the Yuma Indians — those Indians who settled along the Colorado River Valley. Their territory included land on both sides of the river and extended from the Gila River to the mouth of the Colorado River. These desert river people are Hokan speakers related to the Kumeyaay and Chumash. They share the Yuman language with seven other Colorado River tribes, along with Chumash and Kumeyaay. Historically they have been known as fighters, battling the Papago, Apache, and others for control of the river. The river's importance is captured in their creation story, which tells of the god Kumastamxo who traced a course through the desert with the tip of his lance, piercing the earth and forming the Colorado River.

Their continuity as a sizable tribe, still numbering about 2,400 members, can be attributed to their strong spirit and the rewards of locating on the banks of the Colorado River. The Quechan traditionally practiced planting and farming along the banks of the river. Annual flooding deposited rich soil in the low-lying shore areas, creating excellent farming grounds. From early times the Quechan learned how to cultivate and raise crops native to the area such as maize,.wheat, beans, cantaloupes, watermelons, calabashes, and grass seeds. They also grew some cotton and tobacco. The cultivated crops, fish and game, and freely growing edibles, provided the Quechan with a nutritious and replenishable diet.

The Quechan originally built large dwellings made of logs covered with mud on the outside. Or, they lived in semi-subterranean huts lined with grass with straw roofs above ground. The huts were not concentrated in villages, but were scattered extensively along the bottomland of the Colorado River valley. They were grouped into loose bands of about 125 people, but most of the year they lived in small extended families of about 25 people. Each band had its headman. Unlike many of the other Yuman speaking tribes, the bands were sometimes organized into a tribe of 2,000 to 3,000 members who were led by a chief.

The Quechan people preserved their proprietary territory but traveled great distances to visit other people for peaceful trading or to engage in opportunistic hostile activities. Their expeditions went far into Mexico to the south, into Chemehuevi territory to Needles in the north, and to the Pacific Coast in the west. They exchanged pottery and baskets from eastern tribes for shells and fishhooks from the Pacific Coast tribes.

Culturally they have been influenced by their O'Odham (Pima and Papago) and Pueblo Indian neighbors to the east. One of their most significant crafts, learned from their eastern neighbors, was the paddle-and-anvil technique for making pottery, which fused separate pieces of clay to make a pot. This technique was later adopted by the neighboring Kumeyaay and other tribes to the west.

The earliest Spaniards to ascend the Colorado River in 1540 (Hernando de Alarcón) and 1604 (Juan de Oñate) explored the river and the land to the east and failed to report seeing the Quechan who lived exclusively on the west side of the river at that time. The first to mention the Quechan by name was Father Eusebio Kino in 1701-2. Later, Father Francisco Garcés (1771) and Juan Bautista de Anza (1774) befriended their chief because they knew the critical importance of controlling the Colorado River crossing into California. Anza named the chief Salvador Palma, who was known among his own people as Olleyquotequiebe, and took him to Mexico City where he was baptized in the cathedral. Chief Palma provided major support for Anza's expeditions to California.

The Spaniards lost no time in establishing two strategic missions on the river, Concepción and San Pedro Y San Pablo, to control the Indians and guard the crossing. The settlements destroyed valuable croplands and displaced the Indians who had lived there, and the relationship with the Indians gradually deteriorated. The peaceful period ended in 1781 when the Quechan and Chief Palma enlisted the aid of their neighbors, the equally fierce Mohave, and rose up to destroy the two missions, killing the soldiers and priests, including Garcés, and effectively closed the road to California for several decades.

Juan Bautista de Anza opened the overland road to California.

The Quechan maintained their independence for several generations until the Anglo-American invasion, soon after the discovery of gold in California. Fort Yuma was established in 1849 to protect early settlers from the Indians. Later in 1884, the fort was deeded to the Quechan people when Fort Yuma Quechan Reservation was established on the site of the ill-fated Mission Concepción. The reservation today is a 50,000-acre tract, covering portions of California's Imperial County and Arizona's Yuma County. To the south it borders the Mexican states of Sonora and Baja California. Significant geographic features of the reservation are the Colorado River, which flows from north to south, and Interstate Highway 8, which traverses from east to west. The reservation is mostly made up of low-lying desert land and positioned exactly between San Diego and Phoenix, about 180 miles from each.[16]

BROKEN PROMISES, BROKEN NATIONS

This general review of the history of the Indians along the Jackpot Trail has described many instances of abuse and loss of rights. If the reader thinks this was all something that happened a long time ago, think again. Abuse of the Indians and their rights went on through the 20th Century, and in some measure it continues today.

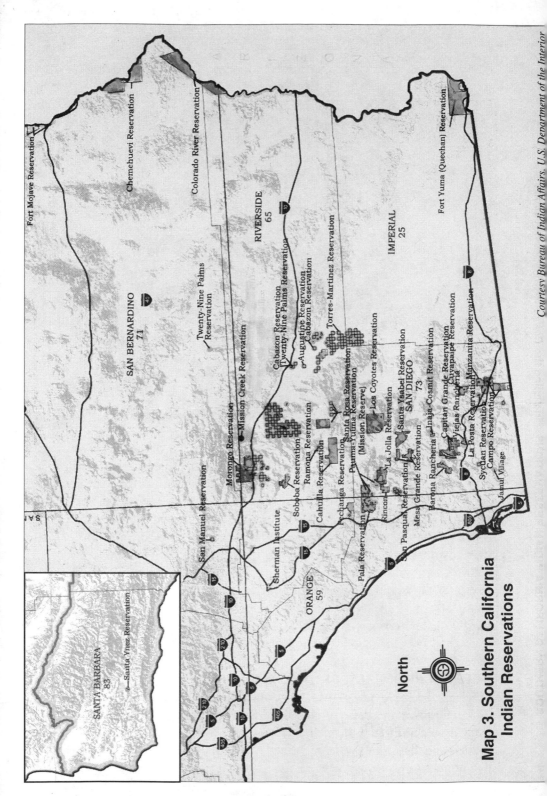

Courtesy Bureau of Indian Affairs, U.S. Department of the Interior

Map 3. Southern California Indian Reservations

North

SANTA BARBARA 83
Santa Ynez Reservation

Fort Mojave Reservation

Chemehuevi Reservation

Colorado River Reservation

SAN BERNARDINO 71

RIVERSIDE 65

Twenty-Nine Palms Reservation

Mission Creek Reservation

Cabazon Reservation
Twenty-Nine Palms Reservation
Augustine Reservation
Cabazon Reservation

Torres-Martinez Reservation

IMPERIAL 25

Fort Yuma (Quechan) Reservation

Morongo Reservation

San Manuel Reservation

Los Coyotes Reservation

Santa Rosa Reservation
Ramona Reservation
Pechanga Reservation
Pauma Yuima Reservation
(Mission Reserve)
La Jolla Reservation
Santa Ysabel Reservation

SAN DIEGO 73

Inaja-Cosmit Reservation

Capitan Grande Reservation

Cuyapaipe Reservation

La Posta Reservation

Manzanita Reservation

Soboba Reservation

Cahuilla Reservation

Rincon Reservation
Mesa Grande Reservation
Barona Rancheria
Viejas Rancheria
Sycuan Reservation
Campo Reservation
Jamul Village

Sherman Institute

San Pasqual Reservation

Pala Reservation

ORANGE 59

22

SOUTHERN CALIFORNIA INDIAN RESERVATIONS -- Including the *Colorado River Reservations**

NOTE: The four Colorado River Reservations are not usually included in the Southern California Reservations; one is located totally in California and the others stretch into Arizona and Nevada. Two California casinos are located on the Colorado River Reservations. Acreage below is for California land only. Resident figures are for tribal and nontribal members who live on reservation land in CA -- nontribal residents sometimes outnumber tribal members.

RESERVATION: (21 gaming reserves)	COUNTY **multi county	GAMING/CASINO: (22 casinos)	INDIAN TRIBE:	TOTAL Acres:	TOTAL Residents:	NOTES: 35 total reservations in So CA
Santa Ynez	Santa Barbara	Chumash Casino	Chumash	125	~250	~100 residents are tribal members
Total: 1 reservation		Total: 1 casino		Total: 125 acres		Santa Barbara County
Chemehuevi Valley*	San Bernardino		Chemehuevi	30,653	~1,100	~150 residents tribal members/enrollmt ~500
Colorado River*	San Bernardino	Havasu Casino	Mohave/Chemehuevi	~21,350	~2,000	~50 tribal members in CA: over 2,300 members in AZ
**Riverside				(See Riv below)		268,691 total acres incl Hopi/Navajo in AZ
Ft. Mojave*	San Bernardino		Mohave	1,000	~200	33,000 total acres CA, AZ & NV/enrollmt 1082
San Manuel	San Bernardino	San Manuel Casino	Serrano	700	~60	
Twenty-Nine Palms	San Bernardino	in Riverside County	Chemehuevi	160	0	400 acres in 2 counties/unoccupied
**Riverside				(not inc. Riv)		
Total: 5 reservations		Total: 2 casinos		Total: 53,863 acres		San Bernardino County
Agua Caliente	Riverside	Agua Caliente & Spa	Cahuilla	33,000	~21,000	~150 residents tribal members/enrollmt ~370
Augustine	Riverside	Augustine Casino	Cahuilla	500	1	total tribal members is 8
Cabazon	Riverside	Fantasy Springs	Cahuilla	1,609	18	total enrollment ~40
Cahuilla	Riverside	Cahuilla Casino	Cahuilla	18,888	~200	
Colorado River*	Riverside		Mohave/Chemehuevi	~21,350	(See above)	the ~2000 residents are in two counties
**San Bernardino				(See SB above)		42,700 CA acres split ~equally in 2 counties
Morongo	Riverside	Morongo Casino	Cahuilla/Serrano	38,000	~1,000	~500 residents tribal members/enrollmt ~1000
Pechanga	Riverside	Pechanga Casino	Luiseño	4,500	~500	~350 residents are tribal members
Ramona	Riverside		Cahuilla	560	~10	
Santa Rosa	Riverside		Cahuilla	11,092	110	
Soboba	Riverside	Soboba Casino	Luiseño/Cahuilla	6,939	~450	
Torres Martinez	Riverside		Cahuilla	15,396	4,150	~150 tribal members residing in both counties
						27,240 total acres in both counties
Twenty-Nine Palms	Riverside	Trump 29 Casino	Chemehuevi	240	0	400 acres in 2 counties/unoccupied
**Imperial						
**San Bernardino						
Total: 12 reservations		Total: 8 casinos		Total: 152,074 acres		Riverside County
Ft Yuma-Quechan*	Imperial	Paradise Casino	Quechan	42,059	~1,470	additional 8,600 acres in AZ, total residents ~2,375
Torres Martinez	Imperial		Cahuilla	11,843	(See above)	(See above)
**Riverside						
Total: 2 reservations		Total: 1 casino		Total: 53,902 acres		Imperial County
Barona	San Diego	Barona Casino	Kumeyaay	7,018	~530	~340 residents are tribal members
Campo	San Diego	Golden Acorn Casino	Kumeyaay	15,480	~350	~230 residents are tribal members
Capitan Grande	San Diego		Kumeyaay	15,750	0	unoccupied
Ewiiaapaayp	San Diego		Kumeyaay	5,460	~30	also called Cuyapaipe
Inaja-Cosmit	San Diego		Kumeyaay	850	~15	
Jamul	San Diego		Kumeyaay	6	~40	
La Jolla	San Diego	La Jolla Arcade	Luiseño	9,098	~390	240 residents tribal members/enrollment ~620
La Posta	San Diego		Kumeyaay	3,700	18	15 residents are tribal members
Los Coyotes	San Diego		Kumeyaay	25,050	~200	~70 residents tribal members/enrollment ~212
Manzanita	San Diego		Kumeyaay	4,590	~70	~30 residents tribal members/enrollment 67
Mesa Grande	San Diego		Kumeyaay	1,803	180	~75 residents tribal members/enrollment 630
Pala	San Diego	Pala Casino	Luiseño/Cupeño	11,950	1574	~400 residents tribal members/enrollment 585
Pauma-Yuima	San Diego	Pauma Casino	Luiseño	5,877	~190	~40 residents are tribal members
Rincon	San Diego	Harrah's Rincon Casino	Luiseño	4,275	~1,500	~150 residents tribal members/enrollment 651
San Pasqual	San Diego	Valley View Casino	Kumeyaay	1,380	752	~112 residents tribal members/enrollment 289
Santa Ysabel	San Diego		Kumeyaay	15,526	~330	250 residents are tribal members
Sycuan	San Diego	Sycuan Casino	Kumeyaay	808	~75	enrollment 120
Viejas	San Diego	Viejas Casino	Kumeyaay	1,609	~400	~200 residents are tribal members
Total: 18 reservations		Total: 9 casinos		Total: 130,230 acres		San Diego County

NOTE: Acreages and reservation populations obtained from BIA, 2000 U.S. Census, info@me.sdsu.edu/research/guides/calindians/calinddict.shtml and www.csusm.edu/nadp/ascnas/screserv.htm -- corrected updates from tribal offices in November 2002
© 2003 Diana Lindsay

Incredibly as late as the 1950s there were movements to terminate Indian tribes and eliminate their claims to reservation lands. Many Indian tribes fought these issues at state and national levels for over two decades before the U.S. passed the Indian Self-Determination Act in 1975. Also in recent times Indians were finally given the right to practice their native religions (American Indian Religious Freedom Act of 1978, amended 1996). Can you imagine, in this great bastion of democracy, where settlers first came to seek religious freedom, the denial of religious practices to Native Americans all those years?

A word should be said for the many Americans who have supported Indian rights over the years. Their devotion to the Indian's cause has helped immensely, but nothing done previously has the potential to help Indians achieve financial independence as much as Indian gaming. The power of the almighty dollar reigns supreme, and with that power Indians can control their future. So far it is working, and their new found wealth is being used with discretion to improve the lives of Indians while also contributing to the well-being of local and state communities. However, be aware that the success of the Indians brings with it resentment and envy from some quarters. Some, including government bodies, covet the Indians' earnings, and others, for various reasons, wish to curtail Indian rights. Unfortunately, Indians will be fighting these battles far into the future.

TRIBAL GOVERNMENTS

From the earliest sources available, it is evident that a democratic form of government traditionally existed in the bands and tribes who selected headmen to lead them. This tradition continues today. There may be some variation from tribe to tribe or band to band, but all are operated in a very democratic fashion. They did not learn about democracy from the white man. Each tribal member of age, usually 21, has an equal vote in all matters. An administrative leadership is elected from the members to serve fixed terms, which may be from two years to five or even more. They also elect a tribal leader, today often called a chairman/chairwoman or chairperson (rather than a chief who is an honorary leader who serves for life). In some tribes the chairman has been re-elected several times and has served for several years. Women are accorded great respect in all tribal matters and frequently hold tribal offices. It is not uncommon to have more women than men in such positions. The tribal council conducts the day-to-day business of the tribe, but if any new matters or substantive issues arise, they are referred to the general membership. Democracy prevails.

CHAPTER 2
SOVEREIGNTY AND
ENABLING LEGISLATION

Sovereignty is a right that distinguishes Native Americans from other Americans. This unique status, recognized by the United States government, is established through treaties, legislation, executive orders, and policies. It is conveyed to successive generations based on established, well-defined land holdings called reservations.

It is inaccurate to say the United States granted or gave sovereignty to Indians. As occupants of the great lands of North America, Indians were de facto owners and had inherent rights over their territory. Unfortunately for the Indians, they did not have the power to assert or successfully defend those rights. After wholesale takeover of most Indian lands, reservations were established in the late 1800s, which finally set aside land that could not be taken by any individual or subgroup. These reservations have been placed in a perpetual trust for the exclusive use of the designated tribe or band.

Sovereignty is an attribute of a nation, such as that of the United States of America. In accordance with the U.S. Constitution, sovereignty is also granted to the states, reserving for the states all rights not specifically given to the federal government. Add to this mix the sovereignty of Indian nations and you have a complex interaction of sovereignties that is confusing and often conflicted, from time to time requiring the intervention of the Supreme Court.

A major contention of Indian governments, which has been upheld by the U.S. Supreme Court, is that states do not automatically have rights to legislate policy affecting Indian lands. This is possible only if the U.S. Congress has granted states specific authority, or if tribes choose to work with the states on matters of mutual interest.

Indians claim that gaming was part of their culture as far back as their legends relate (see "Indian Gaming as a Cultural Tradition" in the Introduction to this book). In modern times Indians witnessed state governments expanding gaming beyond betting at racetracks to include other forms of public gambling such as bingo games, card rooms, and lotteries. They hungered for part of the action and felt, as sovereign entities, they had a solid claim to permit gambling on their lands. From the mid-1900s there were numerous skirmishes with state authorities as Indian tribes expressed their assumed authority with various types of gambling. By the mid-1980s many tribes had established bingo games, starting a movement that state governments and courts were unable to stem.

A landmark court case brought Californians into the debate in 1986 when the U.S. Supreme Court heard *California v. Cabazon Band of Mission Indians, et al*. The opinion of the Supreme Court, issued February 25, 1987, stipulated that if a state permitted bingo and other kinds of gaming such as card rooms, race tracks, and lotteries, they could not bar California Indian nations from participating in like ventures. This decision was a huge step forward for Indian gaming.

The way was then open for Congress and then President Ronald Reagan to set up rules and guidelines that would allow Native Americans to use gaming operations for the purpose of improving their economic status and, thereby, the lives of Indian people. The Department of Justice and the Department of the Interior implemented legislation that clarified issues and established workable regulations. Federal guidelines of the Indian Gaming Regulatory Act (IGRA) of 1988 were intended to settle issues of Indian gaming in reservations across the country. IGRA segregated gaming into three different classes with associated levels of jurisdiction and regulations.

Class I was designated as the social or traditional gaming played in ceremonies, which allotted prizes of minimal value. Class I remains under tribal jurisdiction.

Class II included bingo and similar games, pull-tabs or punchboards, and any nonbanking card games that are not explicitly banned by the state constitution. Nonbanking games would include any card games where players wager against each other, placing wagers into a common pool (pot). These games, falling under tribal jurisdiction, are further regulated through the National Indian Gaming Commission, (NIGC), a regulatory agency created by IGRA.

Class III includes all other forms of gaming that do not fall into the first two categories. Electronic games of chance called for a Tribal-State Compact or agreement, approval by tribal ordinance, and approval of NIGC. All Tribal-State Compacts are ultimately subject to approval by the Secretary of the Interior.

IGRA guidelines were to be used by Native Americans to establish and run gaming centers on their tribal lands. This new revenue source had the potential to provide economic self-sufficiency for bands and tribes whose reservations were fortuitously positioned near population centers and located in states where gaming was permitted. If a state had not already opened the door by authorizing some form of public gambling, Indian entities have no right to initiate gambling in that state.

The real prize for Indian tribes was Class III gaming, the slots and house-banked table games, which are the big draws and big money earners. The Tribal-State Compact negotiated between the state of California and Indian tribes specifically addressed these games and set certain limits, the most significant being: no reservation may have more than two casinos, or have more than a total of 2,000 slot machines.

The compact also directs how income made by tribes having casinos is shared with non-gaming tribes. However, it is not specific about the amount of revenue sharing. This feature is apparently operated on the honor system, and it seems to be working as distributions have been made. It remains to be seen whether equanimity between the "haves" and "have-nots" will continue.

The compact also created a State Gaming Commission to work in concert with individual tribal gaming commissions to oversee operations regarding employment practices, disputes, public liability, and other matters of regulation that all businesses in the state are required to enforce. These include matters of the environment, sanitation, safety, and certain credit practices.

The laws and regulations promulgated thus far have given sufficient rights and latitude for Indian tribes to operate profitably. According to a tribe's financial status, they can start modestly, if necessary, and expand as revenues permit. What has taken place thus far has demonstrated that Indian people and their tribal management are up to the task of taking on these entrepreneurial enterprises and are doing well with them.

After the groundwork was set for tribes to move into Class III gambling, the state of California under the leadership of Governor Pete Wilson sought to restrict the Indians on the basis of state laws then on the books. While the governor was "jaw-boning" the Indians and legislature, a sweeping voter initiative, Proposition 5, was put onto the 1998 election ballot to permit Class III gambling. Large gaming interests in Nevada were the primary opponents, as they anticipated a negative impact on their future earnings. A coalition of Indian communities and related parties were the primary supporters of the proposition. Over $200 million was spent in the largest election proposition media war ever waged in California. For months California voters were bombarded on television and with print ads giving opposing views. They were relieved to put it all behind them when the support for Proposition 5 won with a two-thirds majority.

Even so, Governor Wilson was not ready to capitulate. He petitioned the California Supreme Court to declare the proposition unconstitutional.

Fortunately for supporters of Proposition 5, the same election ushered in a Democratic administration. Governor-elect Gray Davis had early on signaled support for the Indians and had benefited from their campaign contributions.

After the election the governor met with Indian leaders and struck a deal to "make them self-reliant." The deal depended on further consent of voters by way of another ballot initiative (Proposition 1A) scheduled for the year 2000 elections. California voters once again supported the Indian cause, and the rest is history.

Just before this manuscript was completed a significant challenge to Indian gaming rights came before U.S. District Judge David F. Levi contending the granting of monopoly rights to Indians was unconstitutional. Judge Levi ruled, in an extensive examination, that a monopoly granted to tribes on slot machines and Las Vegas style card games did not violate the U.S. Constitution or other statutes that regulate Indian gaming.[17] This issue may wind up before the U.S. Supreme Court, but the decision handed down by the district court will strongly influence the Supreme Court's decision, if they even elect to hear the matter.

Courtesy Sycuan Casino and Resort

Poolside at Singing Hills Resort at Sycuan

CHAPTER 3
WHERE THE MONEY GOES

E very Indian casino can state its case for the economic benefits it brings to surrounding communities, which is in direct proportion to the size of its operation. The greatest impact is from creating new jobs at the casino, 95% or more of which are filled by non-Indians. Money earned by these employees flows back into their home communities. For every 1,000 employees, there is about $25 million in payroll that employees can spend. The purchase of goods and services by a casino to support its own operations has even greater impact. For every 1,000 employees there is about $35 million spent on goods and services, predominantly from nearby communities. According to U.S. Department of Commerce estimates, that translates into the creation of about 1,500 jobs outside the casino. Or to state it differently, for every job created at the casino, there are approximately 1.5 *additional* jobs created.

Some observations about the kind of jobs created might be in order. There are some striking characteristics of the new casino workforce. A large percentage of the employees are young and working at entry-level positions, usually at better wage levels than offered at fast food chains. At the other end of the spectrum, there is a noticeable number of older employees, post 55 or 60 years of age, who are working in positions such as customer service, maintenance, and security. This is a group for whom employment at a fair wage is hard to find. Many people are also finding good jobs as dealers and gaming attendants if they have experience or have been to professional training schools. For other experienced people not trained in the gaming industry there are many administrative jobs being filled. Gaming is a growth industry that is here to stay. It affords thousands of Californians new career opportunities and, unlike the vaunted California high-tech industries, it has a place for many with a modicum of education, skills, and training.

There are many specialty schools in California that provide training for prospective casino game operators. For names and locations of some of the schools go to www.casino-dealers.com. In the San Diego area, Grossmont College will soon be offering a degree program in tribal gaming. It will be the first institution in the nation to offer such a program.[18]

There are serious issues associated with the expanding gaming industry in California, not the least of which is problem gamblers. However, from another point of view, for thousands of workers for whom jobs are hard to find it is an answer to their prayers. It is also a classic example of free enterprise redistribution of wealth. Those with the money to gamble create jobs and income for those in need.

Additional economic benefits come from direct contributions by casinos to local charities, sponsorship and direct advertising, local infrastructure improvement cost sharing, and the distribution of a portion of earning to non-gaming Indian tribes.

Those who speak critically of Indian gaming as having little or no benefit to local communities speak out of ignorance. A common myth is that casino operations do not pay taxes. The fact is casinos, like other businesses, pay millions in payroll taxes, social security, unemployment insurance, and health insurance every year. All their employees are also subject to local, state and federal taxes.

Unlike personal businesses, the net earnings from casino operations belongs to the respective tribal governments, and how this money can be spent is specifically mandated according to the federal Indian Gaming Regulatory Act. The revenues may only be used to:

1. Fund tribal government operations or programs
2. Provide for the general welfare of the Native American tribe and its members
3. Promote tribal economic developments
4. Provide for charitable causes
5. Help fund operations of local governments

Most tribal governments use gaming profits for education, fire protection, law enforcement, cultural preservation, health and dental care, new roads, sewer and water services, and senior care, among other needs, after distributions for business expenses and general welfare.

Another prevalent myth is that Native Americans do not pay personal taxes. The fact is that they pay all taxes required by state and federal law. They pay federal income tax, state income tax, social security taxes, local sales taxes and other taxes that apply to other citizens. The only exemption is for Indians who live on property on federally designated reservations. They are exempt from local property taxes and certain other state taxes, such as sales tax if the product purchased is delivered to the reservation. At the same time, however, they usually do not use the services or infrastructure of local governments.

PART TWO — THE CASINOS

CHAPTER 4
WINNING JACKPOTS

Though some casinos may be small, their jackpots can be huge and payouts frequent. Casino operators know that to lure a steady stream of gamblers — the lifeblood of their existence — they must make good payouts, and they do!

At Barona, Kevin won a megajackpot of $891,356 and Mary won $179,000. Hilda won $380,234 at Harrah's Rincon Casino playing Wheel of Fortune®. At Valley View, a relatively small casino, Cruz hit a progressive jackpot for $1,326,505! These are but a few of the larger jackpots. Every casino has many success stories of big jackpot wins, which they frequently publicize.

PLAYER'S CLUBS

Almost all casinos offer free registration for their version of a player's club. The club provides special benefits for those who gamble frequently, or in large amounts, by keeping track of the amount of their bets and awarding points according to the dollars played. These points can be redeemed for a variety of goods or services, including meals, gift shop items, golf or other available amenities of the casino.

Each casino has its own schedule for its accumulation of points. For some, the player is awarded one point for every $1 of wagering and it may take 1,000 points to achieve a credit of $1. At first this may seem a very small payback — $1 for every $1,000 played. What should be considered, however, is that a dollar wagered will often win several dollars, and those additional dollars of play are all counted, just as if they came out of the gambler's pocket. Also, many casinos have a more liberal reward policy than the $1 for every $1,000 played. A check with the individual casinos will reveal what their reward policy is.

The small wager, occasional gambler may not accumulate enough points to amount to much, but even so, the author recommends that every new visitor to a casino sign up and get a player's club card.

FOR THE NOVICE

When you sign up for a player's club, you will be asked your date of birth and for some, your wedding anniversary. This information goes into the casino's data base, and guess what? When the month of your birthday or anniversary rolls around, you are likely to find cards in the mail from a casino with offers such as a free meal or $5 of free play. If you don't mind mail of this sort, you may want to cash in on the goodies. If for nothing else, the player's club card is a great souvenir, and it's free. Just ask the security person as you enter the casino for directions to the player's club registration or the customer service desk. Most casinos offer a tether cord to attach to your card. This is a very practical safeguard against leaving your card in a machine.

It takes little or no skill or experience to play most casino slot and video games. Each casino has a hundred or more different games with recognizable names such as Wheel of Fortune®, Jeopardy!®, Blondie®, Monopoly® and $1,000,000 Pyramid™. These are all games of chance with no skill required — just the luck of the draw. Machines are categorized by the minimum cost per play: 5¢, 10¢, 25¢, $1 or $5. There are even machines that play for as little as 1¢. (Don't confuse a $5 machine with a 5¢ machine. A few tries could wipe out your bankroll!)

An easy way to steer clear of the wrong denomination of a machine is to observe its "candle." This is the cylindrical shaped object on the top of all slots and video machines. It is used as a call light for an attendant, but it also displays the machine's denomination in color-coded bands. You may not remember all of these, but you should at least remember the color code for your favorite: 5¢ is red, 10¢ is green, 25¢ is yellow, and $1 is blue.

After you select a machine, insert your player's club card. Be sure it registers an acceptance. The digital readout may indicate "Good Luck" and your first name or some other such message. Some machines take coins, but most all games used now take paper money in any denomination up to $100. Once your money is deposited, the machine will register your credits, usually in the lower left corner of the screen. Verify your credit before you start to play.

The old style slot machines had three mechanical spinning reels, accepted only one coin at a time, were activated by pulling a lever, and paid out in coins when a winning combination was displayed across the central line of the machine. Many of today's machines have replaced the mechanical reels with video pictures sorted and displayed at random, which appear in three to five sets of vertical columns and three horizontal rows. A winning line may be in horizontal (three possible) or diagonal direction with up to six additional variations. The player is offered the option of playing from one to nine lines. The other option is the amount of credits you spend per line.

Unless you want to conserve a small bankroll or take time with small bets to get accustomed to the game, it is best to go for the maximum number of lines every time (so you don't miss a winning combination) and select the number of credits per line that you can afford to wager. For example, most 5¢ players select nine lines with one credit (5¢) per line for a total of 45¢ per play. If you

Courtesy Barona Valley Ranch Resort and Casino

A gaming room, Barona Casino

want to wager more heavily, increase the credits per line, up to the maximum if you wish. There is a good argument for playing the maximum bet per machine to qualify for "progressive" jackpots. For example, a 9-line machine may accept a bet of 5 credits (25¢) per line. To go for the maximum on a 5¢ machine, it would cost 5¢ x 9 lines x 5 credits = $2.25 per play.

If you are going to wager the machine maximum, find a machine with a progressive jackpot pool. You can identify these machines by the special banner on top, which will show the amount of money in the current jackpot pool. Depending on the game, this amount may be from a few thousand dollars to over a million dollars. This is where the megabucks are won. The pool, which may involve many casinos, is created from a small percentage of the money paid each time the machine is played. The first person to hit the top winning combination of the machine gets the entire pool if they made the maximum bet.

The other class of slots is the reel type games, which may be video or mechanical, typically the "bars and 7s" games. These are for the more serious players who don't want to be entertained or distracted.

The video games previously described allow the simplest, almost mindless type of gambling, which is what most people enjoy. The next step up in complexity for video games is poker. In this game a five-card hand is displayed on the video screen after the bet is made and the "draw" button is engaged. Video poker is a game of chance as far as the initial hand is concerned, but there is a skill requirement as the player holds or discards certain cards to achieve the best poker hand. Chance again comes into play as the player engages the draw button again to replace the discards. The machine, in perfect random fashion, replaces the discarded cards from the remaining cards of the deck, and adds them to any held cards.

After the second draw, hands that include a minimum of a pair of face cards win back their bet. Higher combinations such as two pair, three of a kind, straights (cards in sequence, i.e., 7, 8, 9, 10, Jack), flushes (all the same suit), four of a kind, straight flushes (in the same suit sequence), and royal flushes (10, Jack, Queen, King, Ace, all of the same suit), earn payouts according to the schedule posted on the machine. The jackpot hand is the royal flush. It happens once in about 650,000 games, but it happens.

There is a definite mathematical science for selecting the keepers to optimize chances for winning in video poker. It is too much for this book to go into, but a few basic suggestions are given below. If you are interested in a thorough understanding, a book such as *Win at Video Poker* is recommended.[19]

Here are some tips gleaned from that book: 1. Holding any pair is better than holding any single card, even an ace. 2. If no pair, hold picture cards. 3. Always hold two pair or any higher combination. 4. If choosing between a pair of picture cards or a four card flush or straight, always keep the pair, unless the four card flush or straight are in order. 5. If choosing between a pair of non-picture cards or a four card flush, always keep the flush. 6. For random cards of ten and under, always re-deal. 7. For two or three cards of a straight or flush, always re-deal. 8. Never hold a "kicker" (a high card such as an ace) with a pair.

There are exceptions to the above, but if the beginning player follows these suggestions, he will do better than the average novice.

A final caution: some machines will automatically select the cards to be held, which you can de-select if the machine choices are contrary to the basic rules stated above or your choices. If you have been dealt a "pat" hand, i.e., every card for a combination, whether a straight, flush, or full house, be certain to "hold" every card before pushing the draw button. If you inadvertently dump a winning hand there is no recourse.

Video poker machines have from one to as many as 50 different hands that you can play, more or less simultaneously. The initial selection/discard is the same for all hands, but the drawn cards are different and distributed at random. Each additional hand played requires another bet. The multiple-hand play adds another measure of excitement and opportunity to win and lose money more quickly.

Many casinos now also have more complicated multiplayer video games such as video roulette, video craps, and video blackjack, which are best left to the more experienced gambler.

In the realm of table card games, the simplest to learn and enjoy is probably blackjack (21). All table games require higher stakes than the lowest wager video games and tend to be more complicated for the novice gambler. Some casinos offer individual instructions during slow periods or have classes occasionally for those that wish to learn the rudiments of a game. Otherwise, there are many good books available at bookstores or your library written specifically to teach all the table games.

Most of the table games are variations of poker. One popular game found at casinos is called Pai Gow. It is an Asian game where players form two poker hands (one of five cards and one of two cards) from seven cards dealt. In Pai Gow the object of the game is to have both of the player's hands rank higher than both hands of the designated banker. Players have the option to place a bonus bet and automatically qualify in three ways to win the bonus. The best five cards qualify for the bonus.

If you are a novice, you may be uncomfortable in a table game you don't understand. You will have less chance to win and your presence may not be welcomed by other players. If you have an interest in learning a table game, try your luck when play is light, when the dealer will have more time to instruct you.

If you have an interest in playing blackjack, you might look for one of the multiple-seat blackjack video games. The seating arrangement and table is much like the real thing except the dealer is a video screen and each player has a replica of a table play station on a video screen. The game is played exactly like the table game and the rules and odds of winning are identical.

Bingo is still offered by many casinos, but it is a vestige of earlier days. For some casinos it is more of a consolation for old patrons than a large revenue generator. It's a moderate way to gamble that especially appeals to seniors. It provides an incentive for getting out of the house and socializing. It is also a game that the novice can pick up very quickly.

Bingo has also come into the technology age. Players can choose the traditional card play or go high-tech. Rather than purchasing a card, which you daub with a marker for each letter/number called, you can use a hand held computer devise, or in some casinos a more standard computer terminal, to play the game. A "buy-in" of $15 for ten games, for example, is credited on the computer unit. After that, it's simple. You just watch the screen and the selections appear automatically when called.

Some casinos offer offtrack betting, another vestige of early days, which strictly speaking is not Indian gaming. It is a state gaming franchise, operated by state employees. The casino gets a cut of the net, which though not large is worthwhile because it draws customers. If you are familiar with betting on horses at the racetrack, this is no difference except the track is replaced by a large TV monitor. Bets can be placed on races across the country as they are being run.

MORE ABOUT THE GAMES

Listing the names of all the video and slot games is impractical. First, there are too many different games, well over 100. Second, the list is always changing as new games are added and older games are dropped or converted. Third, since the business is so competitive, the larger casinos mainly have all the same games. Admittedly, it takes some walking around a casino to find your favorite, but exploring the features of each casino should be a fun part of your first visit. In high stakes areas of large casinos, you'll not find many of the "fun" games such as Wheel of Fortune®, Austin Powers™, or Little Green Men.™

The California market is considered by game makers to favor video slots with a preference for "brand" names and games that have all the "bells and whistles," quite literally, and more exciting features such as bonus spinning wheels, elaborate bonus selection screens, and progressive jackpots. There is also a preference on the part of casino operators for video slots. In addition to their popular appeal, they are more suitable for upgrading or conversion than spinning reel games. Since each machine represents an investment of $10,000 to $15,000, the casinos want to protect their investment from obsolescence.

A WINNER'S EXPERIENCE

Joan, a 68-year-old grandmother from San Diego, won over $250,000 last year. Her winnings, from frequent visits to her favorite local casino, were accumulated from small to medium sized jackpots. Her largest single jackpot was $20,000.

Joan was first introduced to casino gaming when she went to Lake Tahoe to accompany her husband, who likes to ski. With faultless feminine logic, she decided she should be able to spend as much money gambling as her husband was spending for a day on the slopes.

Joan was attracted to video poker because it is interactive and requires some decision making, which helped her pass the time. She hadn't played long on a 5¢ machine before she hit the top pay off, a royal flush. For her, it was a great revelation as she realized gambling wasn't just a way to spend money for entertainment, she could actually make money! That seems very simplistic, but experienced gamblers say the most successful gamblers have a winning attitude while those with the attitude that losing is a certainty will always find a way to make it happen.

Joan's $25 jackpot changed the course of her life. For her, it was a lesson that she could win, and her competitive spirit incited her to question how she could win more. First, she realized her bet could have been larger. If she had played the possible five-fold, 5¢ bet, her jackpot would have been $125. Thereafter, Joan always placed the maximum bet on whatever machine she played. Experts will confirm this isn't just a case of simple multiplication. For progressive pools, you must make the maximum bet to qualify for the big jackpots.

Courtesy Barona Valley Ranch Resort and Casino

Joan shows off part of her take

Sometime later Joan was asked to go with a friend to the casino for bingo. Joan wasn't interested in bingo. She had designs on the video poker games. She had $40 with her that day with which she planned to make more. Joan hadn't been idle, just wishfully thinking about winning. She found a book that taught the basic strategy of winning video poker, and she studied it carefully. It's a fact that video poker has an element of player skill, and Joan wanted all the advantage she could muster.

Whether by good fortune or skill, Joan hit an $800 jackpot that day, and it wasn't long before she was making more regular trips to a casino. Joan contends that if you feel comfortable at a particular casino, you'll probably do best there. She made the rounds of all the casinos within a reasonable drive from home, found her favorite, and visited there frequently.

Joan joined the player's club at the outset and never plays a machine without having her card plugged in. She says it makes sense to take full advantage of all the benefits the casino offers, especially when there is no cost and little effort involved. It doesn't take long before a worthwhile balance of points can accumulate, and somehow, getting that free meal, or whatever, makes the outing all the more enjoyable.

Joan was keeping a positive balance in her gaming kitty, but it was nothing spectacular until January 2001 when she hit a royal flush on a $1 machine for a $12,000 jackpot. That hit encouraged her to move up to the $5 machines, playing a five-fold bet of $25. In February she hit a royal flush for a $20,000 jackpot.

Large payouts are not made directly from the machine you are playing. An attendant will show up with some paperwork. An ID card and other information is required, primarily for tax purposes and compliance with the Title 31 Bank Act for transactions over $10,000. After Joan completed the paper work, she continued to play the machine while she waited for her check. Voilà! Before the check arrived she hit another royal flush for an additional $20,000 jackpot!

Joan's documented double jackpot win dispels any notion that after a big hit a machine is cold. Statisticians say that each play of a game starts fresh with regard to the odds for winning. It has nothing to do with past history; that is what chance is all about.

For the year 2001, Joan reported $257,000 in winnings and paid about $100,000 in taxes. Certainly Joan's experience is exceptional, but it is not rare. Joan's winnings have come from modest to medium-sized jackpots, which she wins by playing frequently and playing as smart a game as possible. She's expecting to win one of the progressive megajackpots anytime now.

Does attitude come into play? Except for the occasional lightning strike luck, a winning attitude may make the difference for those sufficiently experienced to make the best of available odds. And maybe a winner's attitude might even rub off. A church friend of Joan's was making a first trip to a casino and asked Joan for some tips. Her friend called the next day to report she hit a progressive jackpot for $220,000!

USING GOOD JUDGMENT

Most people are content to spend what they can comfortably afford without unduly stressing their budget. They enjoy the excitement and adventure of going to a casino, not only for the gambling but also for the good dining, top rated entertainment, resort accommodations, and other attractions. These are the occasional, moderate, and sensible gamblers that casinos want to attract.

Unfortunately, there is a real possibility that gambling may create a serious problem for some people. Such players do a disservice to themselves, their families, and their communities, and frankly, they are bad business for casinos in the long run. Despite being on the winning end most often, casinos do not want the excessive plungers or compulsive gamblers.

Casinos are on the alert for these problem gamblers. A spokesman at a major casino said they have a team specially trained to spot problem gamblers. They take them aside to suggest counseling and discuss their policy of "voluntary expulsion." This action may only serve to shift the problem to another casino, but if the next casino also detects the problem gambler and does the same, it may cause the person to recognize his weakness and seek help.

There is considerable help available for those who have a problem. Probably the best resource is Gambler's Anonymous. The following is a portion from their mission statement:

GAMBLERS ANONYMOUS is a fellowship of men and women who share their experience, strength and hope with each other that they may solve their common problem and help others to recover from a gambling problem.

The only requirement for membership is a desire to stop gambling. There are no dues or fees for Gamblers Anonymous membership; we are self-supporting through our own contributions. Gamblers Anonymous is not allied with any sect, denomination, politics, organization or institution; does not wish to engage in any controversy; neither endorses nor opposes any cause. Our primary purpose is to stop gambling and to help other compulsive gamblers do the same.[20]

They may be contacted by writing, calling, or e-mailing the following: Gamblers Anonymous, International Service Office, Post Office Box 17173, Los Angeles, CA 90017. Telephone (213) 386-8789 or reach them on the Internet at www.gamblersanonymous.org. For a live counselor 24 hours a day and seven days a week call (800) GAMBLER — (800) 426-2537.

Courtesy Barona Valley Ranch Resort and Casino

New voucher technology found in most casinos

SUMMARY 1 -- ALL CASINOS SUMMARY

Pg.	Casino	Location	Telephone	Age	Gaming sq-ft	Bus Service	Slots/Tables	OTB	Poker Room	Bingo	Food Areas	Hotel	Other Special Features
66	Agua Caliente	Rancho Mirage	760 321-2000	21	35,000	yes	1,140/32		yes	yes	6		Near Palm Desert stores & museum
71	Augustine	Coachella	760 391-9500	21	22,000		349/10				2		Many 1¢ slots
138	Barona	Lakeside	888 722-7662	18	85,000	yes	2,000/52	yes	yes	yes	9	yes	Museum, chapel, golf, gas station
105	Cahuilla Creek	Anza	909 763-1200	21	6,000		207/3				1		Day care center, special events
43	Chumash	Santa Ynez	800 728-9997	18	45,000	yes	2,000/32		yes	yes	1		New casino opens 2003, near Solvang
75	Fantasy Springs	Indio	800 827-2946	21	85,000	yes	1,300/38	yes	yes	yes	3		Museum, bowling center, amphitheater
160	Golden Acorn	Campo	866 794-6244	18	25,000		750/13				2		Truck stop, gas station, mini-mart
126	Harrah's Rincon	Valley Center	877 777-2457	21	45,000	yes	1,500/32				6	yes	Swimming, entertainment, gift shop
87	Havasu Landing	Havasu Lake	800 307-3610	21	6,000		220/5				1		RV park, camping, marina, river, gas
122	La Jolla Arcade	Pauma Valley	760 742-3066	18	500		30/0				1		Water park, RV park, camping, store
55	Morongo	Cabazon	800 252-4499	18	60,000		2,000/46		yes	yes	2		Museum, gas station, Hadley's Fruit
110	Pala	Pala	877 946-7252	21	85,000	yes	2,000/50				6		Cultural Center, mission, gas station
164	Paradise, CA & AZ	Winterhaven/Yuma	760 572-7777	21/18	5,000 CA	yes	675/28		yes	yes AZ	1 AZ		Museum, near Old Yuma & river
117	Pauma	Pauma Valley	877 687-2862	18	35,000	yes	850/20				2		Live entertainment, craps, roulette
97	Pechanga	Temecula	888 732-4264	21	80,000	yes	2,000/63		yes	yes	6	yes	Theater, RV park, gas, mini-mart
48	San Manuel	Highland	800 359-2464	21	80,000	yes	2,000/54		yes	yes	2		Headline entertainment
92	Soboba	San Jacinto	888 772-7626	21	60,000		2,000/54			yes	3		Outdoor concerts and events
60	Spa Resort	Palm Springs	800 258-2946	21	20,000	yes	850/20				2	yes	Museum, spa, Indian Canyons
147	Sycuan	El Cajon	800 2792826	18	120,000	yes	2,000/60	yes	yes	yes	6		Golf, pro shop, tennis, resort
81	Trump 29	Coachella	866 878-6729	21	100,000	yes	2,000/35				6		Headline entertainment
132	Valley View	Valley Center	866 726-7277	21	20,000	yes	780/10		yes		2		Occasional spec events/entertainment
153	Viejas	Alpine	800 847-6537	18	100,000	yes	2,000/72	yes	yes	yes	6		Retail outlet center, RV parks (2)

CHAPTER 5
NORTH BRANCH

SANTA BARBARA AND
SAN BERNARDINO COUNTIES

The North Branch includes the two northernmost casinos to be found in southern California. The Chumash Casino is in Santa Barbara County while the San Manuel Indian Bingo and Casino is 150 miles to the east in San Bernardino County.

The majority of Jackpot Trail travelers heading for the North Branch will be coming from the Los Angeles area. If the Chumash Casino is the first objective, take the Ventura Freeway (U.S. Route 101) west toward Ventura. If your preference is to visit San Manuel first, take I-10 east from Los Angeles, and refer to the directions listed at the end of the Chumash Casino section.

To avoid Los Angeles freeway congestion, don't travel during peak traffic hours. A simple rule for visitors is: don't travel toward Los Angeles, 7-10 a.m., or out of the Los Angeles area, 3-7 p.m.

On Route 101 after Calabasas there is less congestion and some attractive open countryside en route to the Chumash Casino. After passing through Thousand Oaks, the freeway begins a climb at Newbury Park up a grade onto the slopes of Conejo Mountain. Over the crest the highway rapidly descends to the coastal plain near Camarillo. There used to be wide expanses of farmland on both sides of the freeway here, but that was before the onset of commercial development, which now solidly fringes most of the highway from Camarillo to Ventura.

Just beyond Ventura the freeway enters a narrow strip of land alongside the ocean, bordered by the coastal mountains. This region was once a thriving oil field, but now its output is small. You'll see some of the old grasshopper pumps, a few of which might still be working. Look for an idle refinery that is visible from the road, tucked in a small canyon.

From Malibu north all the land was Chumash territory just a couple hundred years ago, back when the tribe's population was about 10,000. Before reaching Santa Barbara, you'll pass through Carpinteria, named after the Chumash craftsmen who once made their seagoing craft there.

Once in Santa Barbara, take SR 154 toward the mountains to Santa Ynez. You will be rewarded with breathtaking views of mountains and backcountry. A few miles out of Santa Barbara, as you are still climbing, you'll find a sign and road off to the right to the famous Chumash Painted Cave. The cave has extraordinary examples of Indian rock art paintings, many of colorful complex designs, which may have you wondering about their purpose.

About 10 miles later, SR 154 enters the Cachuma Recreational Area and its central gem — beautiful Lake Cachuma. Traffic is light along this highway and there are many open stretches that allow the driver an opportunity to relax and enjoy the natural beauty of this exceptional countryside.

As you approach Santa Ynez, look for a turn to the left onto SR 246, which skirts the old section of Santa Ynez and is only a couple minutes away from the Chumash Casino. A brief detour to the right, after turning onto SR 246, rises up a grade into old Santa Ynez. It is definitely worth a visit. The town has been carefully preserved and reconstructed to maintain its early western appearance. Its markets, restaurants, and antique shops look fresh from a Hollywood set, but they are not just façades. You can enter and enjoy their offerings.

The Chumash Casino is on the left side of SR 246, just a short distance beyond the turnoff to old Santa Ynez. With its parking structure and large buildings in close proximity to the highway, it seems a bit out of place in this otherwise picture-book landscape. The property is a nest of large tent structures and temporary boxy buildings, behind which is a large multistory parking garage. You will also note the constricted access due to the construction of the new casino.

Tribal members concede that the casino, which has grown like the house Jack built over the past seven years, is due for upgrading and expansion. The new casino, and later a resort hotel, will be a compliment to the area. The new casino is slated for late 2003.

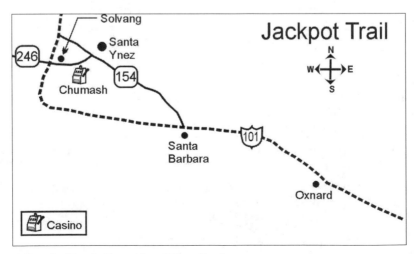

Map 4. North Branch — West Sector

CHUMASH CASINO

Chumash Casino, 3400 E. Highway 246, Santa Ynez, CA 93460
Owned and Operated by: Santa Ynez Band of Chumash Indians
Directions: Freeway 101 north from Los Angeles to SR 154, north
    from Santa Barbara, left onto SR 246 at Santa Ynez
Telephone: (800) 728-9997 toll free
Website: www.chumashcasino.com

Parking: Valet: Yes   **Indoor:** Yes   **Outdoor:** Yes
Bus service: Yes, extensive free buses and municipal buses
Age for admittance: 18
Player's club: Yes, Club Chumash
Nonsmoking area: Yes
Complimentary nonalcoholic drinks: Yes
Alcoholic beverages: No
Gift Shop: No (in new casino, Fall 2003)
Entertainment: No (in new casino, Fall 2003)
Restaurant: Yes, 1: light meals and snacks
Casino size/gaming floor: 80,000/45,000 square feet (new casino fall
    2003)

Table games: 32
Video games and slots: 2,000
Bingo: Yes
Offtrack betting: No
Poker room: Yes

Hotel: No (105-room luxury hotel under construction — scheduled to
    open 2004)
Golf course: No
Special attractions: Near Solvang; numerous wineries and golf
    courses nearby in the Santa Ynez Valley

SUMMARY 2

CHUMASH CASINO

The Chumash Casino, owned and operated by the Santa Ynez Band of Chumash Indians, is located at 3400 Highway 246 in Santa Ynez in Santa Barbara County. It offers Nevada style gaming including video games and slots, table games, and bingo.

TRIBAL AND CASINO HISTORY

For early tribal history, see Chapter 1 in this book. The Santa Ynez Band of Chumash Indians was federally recognized on December 27, 1901, under authority of the act of January 12, 1891. Shortly after, they were granted approximately 135 acres for the establishing of the Santa Ynez Reservation.

For many years the elders of the Santa Ynez Band sought means to improve their economic state, but with little capital or other resources, progress was limited. In the early 1980s they made their first move into gaming with a bingo hall in a tent and metal building. In the late 1990s, with the success of Propositions 5 and 1A, they introduced video games and slots and other card games. In a public address in January 2001 Tribal Chairman Vincent Armenta wrote:

> Today, [we have] eliminated unemployment on our reservation while generating jobs, revenues and taxes for the communities around us.
>
> With our gaming operation, we have become the largest employer in the Santa Ynez Valley and we are still growing and making progress. It is because of our ancestral beliefs that we choose to share and give back to the local community.
>
> In the year 2000, the Santa Ynez Band of Chumash Indians contributed more than $1 million to local organizations that are committed to helping others.[21]

Courtesy Chumash Casino

Rendering of the new Chumash Casino and luxury hotel under construction

A parking structure was completed in 2001, which adds 1,000 parking spaces in a multistory enclosed building located on the backside of the casino facing the highway. There are about 200 additional spaces in the open grounds around the casino. The casino offers free valet parking from its front entrance for those who don't want to do much walking or hunting for a parking spot. Although a free service, it is customary to give the car jockeys a tip of a buck or two.

NEW CHUMASH CASINO

While it's business as usual at the Chumash Casino, visitors can expect to find construction on the property through 2004. An upscale new casino is scheduled to open in October 2003, and a 105-room luxury hotel will open a year later.

The new building will have a ground floor entrance and two upper floors. It is designed to enhance and conform to the area's natural surroundings. It will house the 2,000 slots now in play, substituting the latest models as they are available. The table games will be increased to 50 blackjack and novelty games and a 16-table poker room. A modern 1,000-seat bingo hall/theater will provide ample room for avid bingo players as well as for concerts and special events.

Dining will be significantly expanded to provide a fine dining restaurant, buffet, and a 24-hour café. Club Chumash will expand its services and provide additional perks for VIPs.

During the construction phase, the casino management and staff will do everything possible to ease any inconvenience for guests. They will be offering many special promotions and events for its loyal customers.

Enjoy your time exploring the Chumash Casino and its many games of chance. You might buy one of their unusual poker chips for a souvenir before you leave.

GAMES

The present casino is about 80,000 square feet with about 45,000 square feet of gaming area. There are 24 tables for blackjack and specialty games including Let It Ride®, Triple Shot, and 3-card poker. Table limits are $5-$500. Players may wager on up to three positions at a blackjack table. Dealers hit on soft-17.

The casino attracts many serious poker players and has daily tournaments. The 24-hour poker room has eight tables and a variety of games and stakes including: Stud High Low, Omaha, Hold'Em, 7-card stud, and special no-limit games.

Throughout the casino are the tribe's 2,000 video games and slots. They include the latest and most popular games, many of which offer progressive jackpots. Look for the identifying banner on the top of the progressive jackpot machines. A high limit slot room for players only is located just to the right of the main entrance. The entire rear building of the casino is non-smoking.

Bingo, the tribe's original gaming enterprise, is still very popular. The 730-seat bingo hall with its nonsmoking section is open Monday, Wednesday, and Thursday for high stakes evening games beginning at 6 p.m. There are matinee games on Sunday, starting at 2 p.m. New electronic bingo machines and SHOCK-WAVE™ machines give players the latest high-tech approach to the game. Players can also play bingo while watching TV. Buy-ins are from $20 to $25. There are special events planned frequently for bingo players with prizes as impressive as a new Ford Mustang.

Special promotions such as car and cash giveaways are always going on in the casino and change monthly. Call or stop by to see what's new and make sure you join the player's club — Club Chumash. It's free to join and members enjoy perks such as invitations to special events and parties. Use your card when you play and earn points, which you can redeem for an array of valuable merchandise.

RESTAURANT

The Chumash Café is the only restaurant in the Casino. The food is good and prices are reasonable. The restaurant area seats about 50 people at café style tables. The menu is typical of a diner and not the place to expect gourmet meals, but there are plenty of popular food items to choose from to satisfy your hunger. Seniors (over 55) might want to take advantage of the free breakfast service on Wednesdays, 6-10 a.m. Alcoholic beverages are not served in the casino.

BUS SERVICE

The Chumash Casino management understands they must draw their customers from far and wide since the local community has a very small population. They have committed themselves to providing frequent service from a wide span of locations at no cost to their patrons.

Customers can ride free on Tri-County Buses from Paso Robles, Atascadero, Arroyo Grande, Nipomo, Santa Maria, San Luis Obispo, Pismo Beach, Morro Bay, Lompoc, Goleta, Santa Barbara, Camarillo, Ventura, Oxnard, Santa Paula, Carpinteria, Woodland Hills, Agoura Hills, Canoga Park, and Thousand Oaks.

The casino operates a shuttle service from Santa Maria, Lompoc, and Santa Barbara on a frequent schedule. Ask a guest service representative, located just to the right of the main casino entrance, for a detailed schedule if interested in the free bus service.

The casino also uses tour buses for patrons coming from more distant southern California locations. For the communities of Long Beach, Lakewood, Carson,

Los Angeles, and Inglewood, call (562) 402-0735 for details. For service from Pasadena, North Hills, Simi Valley, and Mission Hills call (818) 893-8598.

Stay as long as you wish, but keep in mind there is another treat in store for you only a few miles away in Solvang. Just continue a few minutes longer on SR 246 and suddenly you will think you have been transported to Scandinavia. This unique village has rightfully been dubbed the "Denmark of America."

Amidst its rolling hills are decorative architectural wonders of European style houses, hotels, motels, inns, shops, and restaurants by the dozen. Plan to stay for a while, perhaps overnight, to fully enjoy its wonders and the delicious foods. Oh, those Danish pastries! Overnight accommodations are plentiful but should be prebooked during the spring and summer seasons. Many popular hotel and motel chains have their own bit of Denmark in Solvang. For web browsers, you can find accommodations on their website — www.solvangca.com.

The second stop on the North Branch of the Jackpot Trail is about 150 miles to the south and east in San Bernardino County. The drive back along U.S. 101 and other freeways will take about two and a half hours if you avoid the rush hour crunches. If you start out after a late breakfast, traffic will be moderate to light. For a bit of change in scenery, go from Solvang directly onto U.S. 101 south. As you approach Los Angeles, U.S. 101 will merge into SR 134 east. Around Pasadena, SR 134 will merge into I-210 east. Just before San Dimas, I-210 heads south, and about three miles farther it crosses I-10. Take I-10 east about 40 miles to SR 30 beyond San Bernardino. Take SR 30 west, which will take you to your destination near Highland. As you enter the Highland area, look for signs leading to the San Manuel Bingo and Casino.

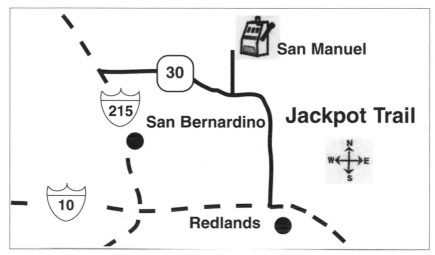

Map 5. North Branch — East Sector

SAN MANUEL INDIAN BINGO AND CASINO

San Manuel Indian Bingo and Casino, 5797 N. Victoria Avenue, Highland, CA 92346

Owned and operated by: San Manuel Band of Mission Indians

Directions: Interstate Highway 10 east from Los Angeles, past San Bernardino, take SR 30 north and west (it turns to the west); exit at Highland Avenue; turn right (east) on Highland Avenue, then left (north) on Victoria Avenue

Telephone: (800) 359-2464 toll free

Website: www.sanmanuel.com

Parking: **Valet:** Yes   **Indoor:** No   **Outdoor:** Yes

Bus service: Yes

Age for admittance: 21

Player's clubs: Yes, 2: San Manuel Player's Club and Bingo Player's Club

Nonsmoking area: Yes

Complimentary nonalcoholic drinks: Yes

Alcoholic beverages: Yes

Gift shop: No

Entertainment: Yes, live, periodically

Restaurants: Yes, 2: café and take-away services

Casino size/gaming floor: 120,000/80,000 square feet

Table games: 54

Slots & video games: 2,000

Bingo: Yes

Offtrack betting: No

Poker room: Yes

Hotel: No

Golf course: No

Special attractions: Check the website for special events and headline entertainers.

SUMMARY 3

SAN MANUEL INDIAN BINGO AND CASINO

The San Manuel Indian Bingo and Casino, owned and operated by the San Manuel Band of Mission Indians who are descendants of the Serrano tribe, is located near Highland to the east of San Bernardino. The reservation land is on the southern slopes of the San Bernardino Mountains. It is one of the oldest Indian gaming enterprises in southern California. Though located in what is known as the Inland Empire, it could be called "L.A.'s Indian casino" for being closest to the megalopolis.

TRIBAL AND CASINO HISTORY

For early tribal history, see Chapter 1 in this book. After the Treaty of Guadalupe Hidalgo, which gave the U.S. government control of California lands, the Serrano encountered Anglo-Americans, sometimes with disastrous results. Many were hunted on the basis of spurious claims of wrong doings and only survived by hiding out in the mountains. Relief came in 1891 when an executive order created the San Manuel Reservation. The name comes from a respected leader, Santos Manuel, who survived the earlier wrath of the white men and aided in the survival of his people.

The reservation was a mixed blessing at best. It gave the band land to claim as their own, but the approximately one square mile parcel on mountain slopes had very little utility for grazing or agriculture.

Tribal leaders have managed some improvements for their members over the years, but the lack of capital and other resources limited their opportunities to make significant improvements until the advent of gaming.

Courtesy San Manuel Indian Bingo and Casino

The San Manuel casino is large, but approaching it by car there is no long-range view to gauge its size. Suddenly it is there, on the right side of the road with a big open parking area opposite. The portico entryway is apt to be crowded with vehicles and rightfully gives the impression of a bustling place.

The original bingo operation opened in 1986 with about 300 employees and became one of the largest bingo operations in southern California, in part because of the high stakes offered. In 1994 the facility was expanded for a card room and to provide space for slots as soon as the legislative hurdles were cleared. Today, at 120,000 square feet, the casino competes with the largest gaming floors anywhere with the maximum number of 2,000 slot and video machines, prescribed by current regulations, and 54 table games.

With economic prosperity has come the opportunity to give back to those who have supported the tribe. The San Manuel Band is a significant contributor to neighboring communities, providing employment for about 1,800 people and generously donating to local projects. The tribal chairman is Deron Marquez.

San Manuel is well structured with open gaming areas having all the games that are allowed in California. The casino enjoys a large clientele (most whom are well acquainted with gambling) and has a very efficient staff. Don't forget to register for a player's club card. Their card is unique. It includes your picture and is a great souvenir (and don't forget to pick up a chip.)

GAMES

The latest video games in San Manuel include Wheel of Fortune®, Jeopardy!®, Monopoly®, $1,000,000 Pyramid™, The Price Is Right™, and many, many more. Plus there is a full selection of video poker games. They offer slots in denominations of 5¢, 25¢, $1, $5, $10, and $25.

Since video keno has always been popular with San Manuel players, the casino offers a variety of machines including Caveman™, Lightning®, Superball, Toucheasy®, and Super Keno, in various denominations.

Slots offer play from traditional 3-line reels up to 45-line multicoin, multi-line video machines. The casino's participation in wide-area progressives offers more fun and excitement and greatly increases the possibility of megajackpots.

All slots and videos use a "ticket in, ticket out" system for play and payouts. They accept cash to begin play and payouts are in the form of a ticket, which may be redeemed for cash or inserted into another machine for additional play.

The casino operates the 54 table games, seven days a week, 24 hours a day. Of these, blackjack is the favorite table game with 29 stations operating during peak times. Everyday there are special offers, bonuses and awards with special prizes on Tuesday and Wednesday. Blackjack tournaments are held monthly with prizes up to $29,000.

Popular promotions include Wacky Wednesdays with cash prizes from $25 to $500 for every blackjack. Wacky Wednesdays are 8-10 p.m. The "Blockbuster" promotions have attracted many players with drawings for $500 to those qualified throughout the day. Freeroll tournaments are held the last week of every month, with qualifying beginning the first of the month.

San Manuel's card room has some of the largest blackjack bonuses in the area. These bonus payouts are offered on a daily basis to players. Back-to-back jackpots are awarded $30 for two, $500 for three, and a minimum of $10,000 for four. The 7-card "Charlie" and 3 sevens earns $100, and the 6-7-8 of the same suit earns $300.

Poker fans can choose from Omaha hi-lo split, Texas Hold'Em and 7-card stud while availing themselves of many opportunities to win special prizes. Both double jackpot and high hand promotions (cash for the high hand of the hour) are held throughout each month. The current month's schedule is posted on the website at www.sanmanuel.com.

Since bingo is in the casino's name, patrons can be sure it gets a lot of attention. There are 1,400 smoking seats and 600 nonsmoking seats in the roomy 40,000 square foot bingo hall. Games are held seven days a week, and everyday is special in some way.

Start times Monday through Friday begin at 6 p.m. with a half hour warm up and a half hour of practice games. Regular sessions begin at 7 p.m. On Saturday and Sunday the Matinee Madness begins at 2 p.m. and the regular session begins at 4 p.m.

Warm-ups, practice games, and weekend matinees are "pay as you play." Cards are sold on the floor for these games and are not included in the buy-in. Additional jackpot games may also be purchased on the floor as well as additional cards for games after the regular session.

All regular games pay a minimum of $1,000 each for single-pack play. Payouts may be larger for special games and promotions. Buy-ins will vary depending on specials and promotions and begin as low as $11.99 for a single pack. Bingo Star electronic bingo machines are available and will play up to 36 cards.

Each year on the third weekend in July, San Manuel Indian Bingo and Casino celebrates its anniversary with two days of special bingo games. The total amount of cash and prizes given away during this weekend has reached one million dollars. Tickets for this special event usually go on sale in June with a discount for early purchase.

The monthly bingo schedule is listed at www.sanmanuel.com or in the bingo mailings. These sources will provide information regarding times, dates, buy-ins, special games, promotions, and coupon acceptance.

San Manuel currently offers two player's clubs: one for bingo players and one for slots and other games. Slot cards can be used to accumulate points for slot play and to enter special contests and promotions throughout the year. These include the annual $250,000 free football contest called SportsWatch, which runs from September to December. Points accumulated for both bingo and slot play can be redeemed for a variety of gifts and prizes. Bingo Player's Club members may also use their cards to obtain discount coupons for bingo play. Discount coupons are available on a monthly basis for those on the bingo mailing list. Coupons are also available for those enrolled in the Bingo Player's Club.

Player's club membership is free with valid picture ID. To be added to the mailing list, call the casino at (800) 359-2464. There is no charge for receiving the mailing.

RESTAURANTS

San Manuel offers a variety of dining choices for players — a snack bar in the bingo hall, a deli near the card room, and a selection of popular Thai dishes in a small café for hungry players.

Breakfast is served in the café from 2:30 a.m. until 10:30 a.m. The north addition of the casino houses A Taste of Italy, an Italian kitchen offering fresh pizza, pasta, and hot and cold Italian sandwiches.

Card players can order food served at their table from a menu. The bingo snack bar serves meals and snacks during playing sessions to over 2,000 bingo players.

Meals and snacks are available 24 hours a day from the other food venues.

ENTERTAINMENT

San Manuel Indian Bingo and Casino offers a variety of live entertainment throughout the year. Acts range from local bands and comedians to headline names like Sinbad, Eddie Griffen, Julio Iglesias, and Willie Nelson. Tickets may be purchased by phone or at the casino's Show Tickets Booth. Prices vary by show and seat location. There is no fixed schedule for major entertainment. Those interested should check the current information posted on the casino's website each month.

BUS SERVICE

The casino offers extensive bus service from local areas and surrounding counties. Details are given at the website www.sanmanuel.com, or those interested may call the San Manual Casino Transportation Department at (800) 331-9536.

If you plan to stay overnight before heading for home, there are numerous accommodations in the area. If you plan to continue on the Jackpot Trail to the Desert Branch, you may prefer to find hotel accommodations in the Palm Springs area.

CHAPTER 6
DESERT BRANCH
RIVERSIDE AND SAN BERNARDINO COUNTIES

B efore embarking on the Desert Branch, you may wish to do some planning, depending on how many stops you will make before heading back
home. The Desert Branch has six casinos in Riverside County in close proximity and the seventh is 190 miles east through the desert in San Bernardino County
on the Colorado River. It's possible, over the course of one day, to visit all six
casinos in the Palm Springs and Indio areas, but it won't give you much time to
explore and enjoy the special attributes of each, let alone the local attractions.

You may wish to stay overnight one evening or more in Palm Springs where
accommodations are plentiful and where you can enjoy many other local attractions. Or you may wish to stay overnight near the Colorado River, in the
Lake Havasu City area, across the river in Arizona. On the other hand, you may
be the type inclined to just wing it and work things out as you travel. That may
work, unless you hit a peak travel time and can't find a hotel or motel vacancy.

We consider the starting point for most travelers on the Jackpot Trail to be
from the west, out of the Los Angeles basin. If you come from more northerly
or southerly points, take whatever route brings you to Interstate 10 east. After
going beyond San Bernardino County on I-10, you will enter the Desert Branch

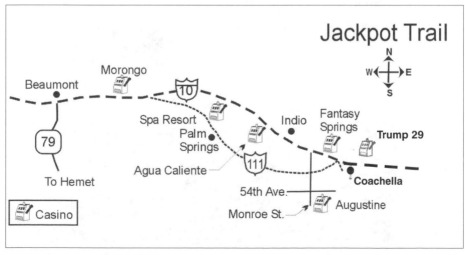

Map 6. Desert Branch — West Sector

in Riverside County. As you continue eastward after Beaumont and Banning, keep a sharp lookout for the exit to Cabazon — the turnoff to Casino Morongo.

Cabazon has other attractions too, not the least of which is one of the largest outlet centers in the country. The stores stretch for more than three-quarters of a mile, all arrayed on the north side of the freeway. At the turnoff on the access road is the Morongo Shell Oil gas station. You may wish to fill up after your visit to the casino, to take advantage of the player's club discount of 10¢ off every gallon of gasoline purchased.

The casino cannot be missed as it dominates the high ground on the north side of the road. Going past the casino to the east, don't be surprised to see a couple of huge dinosaurs that were created by the late Claude Bell. Also nearby is the Hadley's Fruit Orchard outlet. The oldest Indian museum in California — the Malki Museum — is on the Morongo Reservation. You may want to check out these attractions before or after your visit to the casino.

Courtesy Spa Resort Casino

Desert dining at Spa Resort Casino

CASINO MORONGO

Casino Morongo, 49750 Seminole Drive, Cabazon, CA 92230
Owned and operated by: Morongo Band of Mission Indians
Directions: Interstate Highway 10 east from Los Angeles, turn off at
   Cabazon exit
Telephone: (800) 252-4499 toll free
Website: www.casinomorongo.com

Parking: **Valet:** Yes   **Indoor:** No   **Outdoor:** Yes
Bus service: No
Age for admittance: 18
Player's club: Yes, Morongo Winner's Club
Nonsmoking area: Yes
Complimentary nonalcoholic drinks: Yes
Alcoholic beverages: Yes
Gift shop: Yes
Entertainment: Yes, Friday & Saturday, 9 p.m. until 1 a.m.
Restaurants: Yes, 2: fine dining, café
Casino size/gaming floor: 100,000/60,000 square feet

Table games: 46
Slots & video games: 2,000
Bingo: Yes
Offtrack betting: No
Poker room: Yes

Hotel: No
Golf course: No
Special attractions: Other Morongo enterprises nearby include Malki
   Museum, Hadley's Fruit Orchard, A&W and Coco's restaurants,
   and a Shell service station with convenience store.

SUMMARY 4

CASINO MORONGO

C asino Morongo, located on the Morongo Reservation in Cabazon, is owned and operated by the Morongo Band of Mission Indians. The casino can certainly boast about its great visibility and impressive architecture. It is located on the north side of Interstate 10 about 20 miles west of Palm Springs and is within a comfortable driving distance from the Inland Empire and Los Angeles.

TRIBAL AND CASINO HISTORY

For early tribal history, see Chapter 1 in this book. Members of the Morongo Band are mostly descendants of the Cahuilla tribe; others are from the Serrano and Cupeño tribes. According to the *Malki News*, the newsletter of the Malki Museum, "Morongo is the Anglicization or latinization of the word Maarringa' from the Serrano language. Maarringa'yam are the people who speak the Serrano language known as Maarringat."[22] Over the years the Indian languages blended some and have been largely supplanted by Spanish and English.

Tribal members survived through the mission and subsequent periods by farming and raising livestock on reservation land. They harvested trees for

Courtesy Casino Morongo

construction lumber and sold other natural resources found on the reservation, such as peat and asbestos. Some worked as laborers on nearby "rancheros." Executive orders in 1877 and 1881 set aside lands for the Morongo Reservation, now totaling about 38,000 acres — one of the larger reservations in southern California.

The Morongo, numbering about 500 members, have had a focus on education as the way to preserve their heritage and improve their livelihood. Since the 1950s many tribal members advanced their education and found employment outside the reservation, many at professional levels. These modern-day Indians have been instrumental in guiding the band's welfare and economic development.

In 1970 the Morongo Health Clinic opened to serve all Riverside County reservation residents. The clinic is operated by the U.S. Indian Health Service in conjunction with the San Gorgonio Hospital in Banning.

The reservation has many valuable resources such as quantities of good water, large acreages suitable for agriculture and grazing, and processed sand and gravel. Over the years the tribal members studied many proposals for development of their land adjacent to the freeway. For now they are content with their casino, auto service station, Hadley's Fruit Orchard, towing service, paint and body shop, and roadside feed store businesses.

The tribal council is a seven-person board including the chairman, Maurice Lyons. The board manages all tribal business. The council is elected to two-year terms by the general membership — those 21 years of age and older.

The Morongo Band was party to the landmark lawsuit that resulted in a decision by the U.S. Supreme Court in 1987 that set the stage for full-scale Indian gaming. Even prior to that, the Morongo tribal council had initiated plans to enter into gaming with the opening of a bingo hall in 1983. This foundation prepared them to move into Las Vegas style gambling once legislative issues were settled.

In 1995, with confidence in the future of gaming, the Morongo Band invested $6 million for a 40,000 square foot casino expansion. It was a remarkable commitment at the time, but it now pales in comparison to many investments of $100 million and more, including those in excess of $250 million by Barona and Pechanga. Casino Morongo was one of the pioneers and earliest large-scale successes, thereby encouraging others to make greater investments. Morongo also underwent a second expansion of 40,000 square feet to bring it to its current size of about 100,000 square feet. The casino employs about 1,800 people, making it one of the largest economic enterprises in Riverside County.

The gift shop, which is adjacent to the main entrance of the casino, has a good selection of cap and T-shirt logo items and many tribal collectibles including ceramics, pottery, baskets, jewelry, dream catchers, and Native American dolls. It is open 9 a.m. to 5 p.m., Monday through Thursday, 8 a.m. to

Courtesy Malki Museum

Malki Museum

11 p.m. on Friday and Saturday, and 8 a.m. to 4 p.m. on Sunday. All major credit cards are accepted.

MALKI MUSEUM

The first Indian-run museum on a southern California reservation was the Malki Museum, founded in 1964 to promote scholarship, cultural awareness, and understanding of southern California Indian tribes. The name Malki is a Cahuilla word that means "dodging." The Serrano word for Malki is Maarrkinga', from which the name Morongo derives.

The Malki Museum collects and displays materials from all local Indian groups. It is located one mile north of the casino at 11-795 Fields Road on the Morongo Reservation. Call (909) 849-7289 for hours of operation and information about classes and activities.

GAMES

Morongo is a leader in the casino industry. It has the latest and most popular games in inventory. The slots are continually upgraded as new models are available. Morongo has the maximum 2,000 slots with games such as Wheel of Fortune®, Popeye®, Scrabble®, Monopoly®, and 99 Bottles of Beer®, plus dozens more name brands, video poker games, and all the big jackpot progressive machines in reel slots and videos. There's no shortage of machines in various denominations either, although on a busy weekend or holiday a gambler may have to come early or be patient to get a seat at their favorite machine. There's big action at Morongo too. Casino Morongo slot players have won as much as $65 million in a single month.

With 46 table games available, there is a good selection of games and stakes. As in most casinos, blackjack dominates and is supplemented with Pai Gow, mini-baccarat, Let It Ride®, and 3-card poker with a progressive jackpot — the only one of its kind. The casino's poker room also offers Texas Hold 'Em, 7-card stud (high only), and Omaha hi-lo split.

The jackpots are not just on the slots either. The poker room offers "easy qualifying jackpot hands" and gives away thousands every month to jackpot winners. Last year over $15 million was paid out in jackpots, bonuses, promotions, and giveaways.

Casino Morongo is not about to forsake its roots in bingo gaming. It is still very much alive and paying off with great prizes. The bingo hall is open Wednesday through Sunday with prizes up to $1,000 every day. Weekday games begin with the early bird session at 6 p.m. On Saturday there is a 2:30 p.m. matinee, and the evening session starts at 6 p.m. The single Sunday session is at 2 p.m. Most buy-ins are for $20.

The Winner's Club is a win-win situation that costs nothing to join and accrues great benefits for regular players. Members are guaranteed to earn "Cash-Back" points on slots. For each 500 points players get $5 cash back. Members can spend their card dollars at the restaurants and receive other benefits such as invitations to special events and parties, exclusive promotions, and a 10% discount on gift shop merchandise. Here's a bonus you'll not find with other member's clubs — with the Winner's Club card members can get a 10¢ discount on each gallon of gas when filling up at the Morongo Shell service center.

RESTAURANTS

Casino Morongo offers two dining choices to suit their customers' need: Café Serrano and the West End Café. Café Serrano is the more upscale of the two and serves a good selection of salads, seafood, prime ribs, and steaks, along with some interesting oriental dishes to appeal to more diverse tastes. They say you can get freshly prepared wor wonton soup that will rival anything from Chinatown. You may also enjoy beer, wine, and cocktails with your meal as you relax in the comfortable surroundings. The restaurant is open Sunday through Thursday from 7 a.m. to 10 p.m. and from 6 a.m. to midnight on the weekend.

For more casual dining and foods and service more oriented to those on the go, the West End Café is the place to dine. You can enjoy quick snacks or more substantial burgers and sandwiches along with your favorite beverages 24 hours a day, seven days a week.

Just another few miles east on I-10, is the Route 111 turnoff to Palm Springs. The logical next stop on the Desert Branch is the Spa Resort Casino located in downtown Palm Springs. It is just one block north of Route 111 (that becomes North Palm Canyon Drive), the main street of Palm Springs. The Spa is located one block to the left (east) between Andreas and Tahquitz Canyon streets.

SPA RESORT CASINO

Spa Resort Casino, 100 N. Indian Canyon Drive, Palm Springs, CA
  92262
Owned and operated by: Agua Caliente Band of Cahuilla Indians
Directions: Interstate Highway 10 east from Los Angeles, exit High-
  way 111 to Palm Springs (after Cabazon), continue onto N. Palm
  Canyon Drive, left on Tahquitz, the Spa is one block to left
Telephone: (800) 258-2946 toll free
Website: www.sparesortcasino.com

Parking: **Valet:** Yes   **Indoor:** No   **Outdoor:** Yes
Bus service: Free local service from Palm Springs hotels and airport
Age for admittance: 21
Player's club: Yes, Club Paradise (also good at Agua Caliente Casino)
Nonsmoking area: Yes
Complimentary nonalcoholic drinks: No
Alcoholic beverages: Yes
Gift shop: Yes, off hotel lobby
Entertainment: Yes, live from 9 p.m. daily
Restaurants: Yes, 2: steakhouse and bar & grill
Casino size/gaming floor: 40,000/20,000 square feet

Table games: 20
Slot & video games: 850
Bingo: No
Offtrack betting: No
Poker room: No

Hotel: Yes, 230 rooms and suites
Golf course: No
Special attractions: Full-service European style spa for men and
  women; Agua Caliente Cultural Museum, 219 S. Palm Canyon
  Drive; the Indian Canyons Heritage Preserve; Tahquitz Canyon
  Visitors Center

SUMMARY 5

SPA RESORT CASINO

The Agua Caliente Band of Cahuilla Indians own and operate two casinos in the Palm Springs area, the Spa Resort Casino and the Agua Caliente Casino. They are the only tribe or band in southern California to take advantage of the gaming regulation that permits two casinos per reservation. The band's widespread holdings spans two distinct markets: the Spa Resort Casino serves traditional Palm Springs and the Agua Caliente Casino serves the newer developments surrounding the Rancho Mirage area.

TRIBAL AND AREA HISTORY

For general history of the Cahuilla, see Chapter 1 in this book. Anthropologists believe that part of the Desert Cahuilla Indians retreated into the various canyons surrounding Palm Springs — Palm, Murray, Andreas, Tahquitz, and Chino Canyons — when freshwater Lake Cahuilla dried up over 500 years ago. The Indians, however, take exception to this theory. They state that they have always been here since they were created. It was from their hot water spring that this group of Cahuilla Indians took their name of "Se-khi" meaning boiling water. Later the Spaniards put the band's name into their own language as Agua Caliente.

Courtesy Spa Resort Casino

The Agua Caliente people, because of their remoteness from the coastal areas, were spared much of the debilitating effects of the coming of the white man in the late 1700s. It was not until about 1860 that the white intrusion took its toll when massive outbreaks of smallpox and measles decimated the band's population.

In 1876 the Agua Caliente Reservation of 52,000 acres was established by federal order deeded in trust. However, the canny bureaucrats wanted to provide access through the area for the southern California railroad. As in other parts of the country, they created checkerboard patterns of land ownership, which later was negotiated by the parties for necessary right-of-way. About 6,700 acres of the reservation's 52,000 acres occupy the area now known as Palm Springs. The city was built around the Agua Caliente Reservation. The Spa Resort Casino occupies a portion of the reservation land. Other parcels in the downtown area are leased. The majority of their land is in several canyons in its original pristine state.

The most spectacular preserve is Tahquitz Canyon, to the south of downtown. The other Indian canyons — Palm, Andreas, and Murray — are more to the west and south of downtown Palm Springs. All are places of great natural beauty with some of the largest natural palm oases in the world. In the springtime and early summer the canyons are a picture paradise. It is a treat for the eyes and a surefire opportunity for videos and still pictures. Admission fees range from $6 to $12.50 depending on the canyon visited. Admission for children is $2. Regularly scheduled tours are also available.

There is no better place to become acquainted with the cultural history of the Agua Caliente Indians than in Palm Springs. Visit the Agua Caliente Cultural Museum and gift shop at 219 S. Palm Canyon Drive, not far from the Spa Casino. They have an exceptional collection of artifacts and a full-scale re-creation of the native Indian's dwelling called a *kish*. Indian native crafts and other gift items are sold. A large museum facility is slated to be opened soon (November 2005) in the Indian canyons.

The community of Palm Springs also has a rich and colorful history from the late 1920s and 1930s when the Hollywood crowd discovered it. Charlie Farrell's Racquet Club was a gathering spot for the likes of Clark Gable, Errol Flynn, Humphrey Bogart, Lauren Bacall and many more top entertainment and film stars. A bit later Bob Hope came to Palm Springs and has remained as the entertainer icon of the area. Hope's flying saucer-shaped home on the ridge south of the city is one of the better known landmarks of the area. Other well known celebrities who made the area their home include Frank Sinatra, Dinah Shore, Kirk Douglas, and Gerald and Betty Ford.

In 1977 the Agua Caliente Band of Cahuilla Indians and the City of Palm Springs entered into a cooperative agreement for land use development of certain tribal lands. In 1989 the Agua Caliente Development Authority (ACDA) was formed to guide the tribe's future economic development. Development of tribal lands must have the approval of both the city planning commission and the Agua Caliente Development Authority. The tribe has similar cooperative agreements with Cathedral City, Rancho Mirage, and Riverside County. Chairman Richard Milanovich and other members of the council have provided leadership in the development of these tribal enterprises.

CASINO HISTORY

In 1995 the Spa Resort Casino opened in what was formerly the ballroom of the Spa Hotel. The appearance of the Spa Resort Casino from the street is deceiving. It still looks much like the hotel it has been for many years, except for the modest casino entrance to the left of the lobby. Only when driving around to the back does one notice the tent type expansion. The casino is incorporated into the hotel, creating a unique casino experience. After a strenuous workout on the tables or slots, players can enjoy a complete European style spa to pamper their bodies. There is also fine dining and a cocktail lounge only a few steps away. The gaming area is relatively small by today's standards, even after the addition of a tent-type structure adjacent to the hotel lobby.

Going from the casino in the lobby to the tent on the outdoor route takes one past the hot water therapy pools and a large swimming pool. It is tempting to contemplate a dip on a hot day, but the pools are only available to hotel guests. The atmosphere is comfortable, friendly, and relaxed, which many find especially inviting. Others more accustomed to the typical casino may be a bit surprised by the resort hotel environment. In any case, it is a positive and memorable experience for travelers on the Jackpot Trail.

Plans are currently underway for a new Spa Casino facility across the street that is scheduled for completion at the end of 2003.

GAMES

The 24-hour Spa Resort Casino has the exciting table games and slots today's gamblers are looking for with 850 slots and 20 table games. The multidenominational reel slots and video games include most of the current favorites such as, Wheel of Fortune®, Regis' Cash Club™, Monopoly®, Yahtzee®, and many more. Video poker games of single-hand and multiple-hand of various denominations can be found in clusters around the casino floor along with the expected mix of progressive jackpot machines in both slots and videos.

Table game players will find what they are looking for with multiple 6-deck blackjack tables, the popular Let It Ride® option, and many varieties of poker games such as Omaha, 7-card stud, Texas Hold 'Em, and Pai Gow played at different stakes levels. The casino also keeps up player's interests with daily drawings, bonuses and prizes.

Their player's club, called Club Paradise, provides valuable points redeemable for meals, hotel stays, golf, logo merchandise, spa packages and more.

Membership is free and is available at Agua Caliente Casino and the Spa Resort Casino. Points can be earned and converted to prizes at either location. Players earn one point for every dollar of play, and for each 1,000 points accumulated, you earn the equivalent of $1 toward merchandise and meals.

HOTEL

The luxury resort hotel has 229 finely furnished guest rooms with king or queen size beds, five one-bedroom suites, junior suites, and the presidential suite with its private terrace and outdoor whirlpool. Guests may enjoy the full-sized, fresh-water swimming pool at a comfortable temperature or take a hot (98°F) or extra hot (102°F) therapeutic dip in mineral waters in two smaller pools.

This is a far cry from the original and quaint hot springs and bathhouses that the tribe ran for many years prior to the construction of the hotel. Many people came to the healing waters for their curative properties and still do.

The full-service spa has 34 private whirlpool tubs with waters from the hot natural underground mineral springs that made the spot famous. This $30 "Taking of the Waters" is claimed to be a treatment "par excellence" that leaves your mind and body thoroughly refreshed, relaxed, and rejuvenated. Whether the famous waters do the trick or not, casino-goers might enjoy this unusual body pampering break, and they'll surely have something to talk about!

The spa, which caters to both men and women, offers a wide variety of massage arts. They also offer manifold skin care and body treatments from the usual to the exotic, such as a seaweed body mask. For those uncertain about deciding what to have done, the spa offers daily treatment packages from $220 to $410.

Courtesy Spa Resort Casino

The pool at Spa Resort Casino

Hair salon stylists can give you the "stars" look or replicate your usual style while doing manicures and pedicures to add the finishing touches.

Hotel guests more inclined to "do it yourself" workouts can use the complimentary fitness center, which is fully furnished with a range of cardiovascular and strength training equipment and free weights. Personal training instructors are available upon request. A complimentary guest activities program offers group instructions in yoga, tai chi, body sculpting, water aerobics, and more. Hours are 7 a.m. to 7 p.m.

RESTAURANTS

In a warm, friendly atmosphere, the Steakhouse at the Spa Resort Casino offers big succulent steaks, fresh seafood, great appetizers, and desserts. This restaurant is only open in the winter season from September through May, and reservations are definitely needed. Hours are 5-10 p.m. Call (760) 778-1515 for reservations.

The Agua Bar & Grill is open seven days a week year-round, 7 a.m. to 10 p.m. They offer a full range of meals and snacks. Dine indoors or on the patio. This has been a favorite gathering spot in Palm Springs for more than 40 years. There are special food themes nights and brunches. Reservations are suggested even in the off-season. For reservations call (760) 778-1515.

The lobby Cahuilla Coffee Bar is a handy spot for a quick cup of coffee or a light snack if you are not in the mood for more.

ENTERTAINMENT

The Moonlight Magic series of outdoor concerts is presented in the winter season in the parking area adjacent to the hotel. Temporary staging and seats for as many as 3,000 concert goers are provided so audience members may enjoy top name entertainers. For year-round casual entertainment the lounge at the Agua Bar & Grill has a popular piano bar where interesting people entertain.

BUS SERVICE

The casino provides free bus service within Palm Springs to and from major hotels and the Palm Springs Airport. The shuttle leaves for the northern route on the hour, and for the southern route on the half hour from 4 p.m. to midnight. Call (800) 258-2946 for details of stops and times.

The next stop is the Agua Caliente Casino. It is located near I-10 in Rancho Mirage. The most direct route from the Spa Resort Casino is via Ramon Road. Go a few blocks south of the Spa, turn left on Ramon and continue for about six miles. It can also be reached very easily from the I-10 freeway as you travel east beyond Palm Springs into Rancho Mirage.

AGUA CALIENTE CASINO

Agua Caliente Casino, 32-250 Bob Hope Drive, Rancho Mirage, CA 92270

Owned and operated by: Agua Caliente Band of Cahuilla Indians

Directions: Interstate Highway 10 east from Los Angeles, Ramon Road exit in Palm Desert, one block south of the freeway on Bob Hope Drive

Telephone: (760) 321-2000

Website: www.hotwatercasino.com

Parking: Valet: Yes   **Indoor:** Yes   **Outdoor:** Yes

Bus service: Free local service from Palm Springs hotels and airport

Age for admittance: 21

Player's club: Yes, Club Paradise (also good at Spa Resort Casino)

Nonsmoking area: Yes

Complimentary nonalcoholic drinks: No

Alcoholic beverages: Yes

Gift shop: Yes

Entertainment: Canyons Lounge, live nightly; Cahuilla Showroom for top name entertainment

Restaurants: Yes, 6: gourmet, steakhouse, buffet, deli, pizza, ice cream & coffee

Casino size/gaming floor: 50,000/35,000 square feet

Table games: 32

Slot & video games: 1,140

Bingo: Yes

Offtrack betting: No

Poker room: Yes

Hotel: No

Golf course: No

Special attractions: Rancho Mirage and Palm Desert restaurants and stores, Living Desert Museum in Palm Desert

SUMMARY 6

AGUA CALIENTE CASINO

The Agua Caliente Band of Cahuilla Indians own and operate this casino and the Spa Resort Casino in Palm Springs. In addition to being in closer proximity to the rapidly growing desert population, it also takes advantage of direct access to the I-10 at Ramon Road. The casino's exterior architecture is impressive and complements the desert setting.

TRIBAL HISTORY

Refer to the Spa Resort Casino for information common to both.

CASINO HISTORY

The Agua Caliente Development Authority, which successfully developed the Spa Resort Casino, understood its limitation as a casino and decided to up their ante in gaming with an additional casino. Whereas the Spa Resort Casino has the traditional look of an older, well established resort property, the new casino is modern, spacious, and posh. Its slogan, "Play with Style," sets the tone for this playground for affluent visitors to Palm Springs. Of course, this is California where there is no particular dress code, and everyone over 21 is welcome.

The Agua Caliente Casino provides one of the largest nonsmoking areas, perhaps the largest in California. It adjoins the smoking area with no intervening wall, but there is little or no smoke carryover. Even in the smoking areas, the air seems very fresh, no doubt assisted by high ceilings and good air

Courtesy Agua Caliente Casino

movement systems. While there, you may want to check out the Grand Palms Buffet and the five other restaurants.

The Agua Caliente Casino is in close proximity to the present day action of the desert, a lot of which has moved from Palm Springs eastward to the Palm Desert area along Highway 111. Many of the best restaurants and boutique shops are found on El Paseo in Palm Desert, the "Rodeo Drive" of the wintering rich and famous. There is also a large regional shopping center across the highway from El Paseo for those who like to combine shopping with their casino visits. Also nearby is the Living Desert Museum on Portola.

This modern upscale casino opened in April 2001. According to the Tribal-State Compact, a total of 2,000 slots and videos are allotted per reservation. Since there are about 850 at the Spa Resort Casino, that leaves the balance of about 1,140 for the Agua Caliente Casino (ACC). There is no restriction on the total number of table games.

This opulent casino, designed by Las Vegas Strip architects who no doubt had the Palm Springs winter season crowd in mind, presents a classy surrounding for its patrons. The casino floor has over 35,000 square feet for gaming, approximately one-third for nonsmoking patrons.

GAMES

Players will find the latest and best reel slots, video machines, video poker, progressives, and table games at the ACC. For the poker enthusiasts there are 10

Courtesy Agua Caliente Casino

The slot machines at Agua Caliente

tables in the nonsmoking poker room, many blackjack tables of varying limits and 20 other gaming tables for Caribbean Stud®, Pai Gow, 3-card poker, mini-baccarat, etc. The Primrose Room features high denomination slots, table games, and a full-service bar and satellite television for its occupant's enjoyment.

Bingo is big at the ACC with its plush, 15,000 square foot bingo hall. Sessions are held Saturday through Thursday (none on Friday) with starting times of 12 noon, 3 p.m., and 7 p.m., Monday through Thursday, and 2 p.m. and 7 p.m. on Sunday. They offer cash prizes up to $1,000 for game winners and many other cash awards for a wide variety of special pattern cards. Regular buy-ins are $15 with some as low as $2 for early and late games.

The player's club, Club Paradise, is free and can be used at both Agua Caliente Casino and the Spa Resort Casino. Points can be earned and converted to prizes at either location. Players earn one point for every dollar of play, and for each 1,000 points accumulated they earn the equivalent of $1 toward merchandise, meals, hotel stays, golf, logo merchandise, spa packages and more.

RESTAURANTS

The Agua Caliente Casino has six restaurants, fine dining to casual, that offer food selections to please any appetite.

Prime 10 Steakhouse is not just a steakhouse. It serves seafood, duck, chicken, and for the discriminating vegetarian, dishes such as ginger-seasoned grilled tofu steak. Top grade USDA prime steaks are cooked to customer satisfaction and served with appetizing sauces. The unusual dining atmosphere is created by impressive décor with vivid woods and an African motif. Hours are 5-10 p.m. weekdays and 5-11 p.m. on weekends. The restaurant, which seats 165, is available for special functions.

Maraskino is an active, upbeat dining venue complimented by spectacular desert views and hand-painted murals that adorn the walls. Their menu features an eclectic collection of steaks and chop offerings and specialty Spanish tapas filled with savory meats. They also offer pastas, pizzas, salads, and sandwiches for light snacks to full meals. Open daily for lunch and dinner from 11:30 a.m. to 10 p.m. and until 11 p.m. on weekends, check out their bar at happy hour 3-6 p.m. when all tapas are 50% off.

Grand Palms Buffet is a large, well-appointed, and comfortable dining area where you can eat to your stomach's delight. An array of international foods from Mexico, Asia, and Italy, plus good old home country favorite entrées, salads, and sumptuous desserts are served. The buffet is open for breakfast, lunch, and dinner, and for the night owls, a featured "Moonlight Dining" session is open from midnight to 5 a.m. Specialty buffets include "Lobster Wednesdays," when customers can get a one pound lobster for only $5 when purchasing the regular dinner buffet. The "Seafood Extravaganza" is on Friday night. The "Prime (rib) Experience" is on Saturdays, and topping off the week is the "Glory Days Champagne Sunday Brunch" from 11 a.m. to 4 p.m. Buffet prices are $6.95 for breakfast, $9.95 for lunch, and $19.95 for dinner.

The Desert Eatery Court is the place for favorite fast foods. Diners on the go can select from many deli items at New York's Stage Deli open from 8 a.m. to 11 p.m. Mama's Pizza is open from 11 a.m. to 11 p.m., and desserts of ice cream dishes with designer coffees and other beverages are available at Scoops & Brew which is open from 7 a.m. to 11 p.m.

ENTERTAINMENT

The Cahuilla Showroom has brought such diverse entertainment as Wynonna Judd, David Brenner, and championship heavyweight boxing to the desert. Committed to offering the best in headline entertainment, this intimate show-room boasts a state of the art sound system and seating for up to 1,000. For information on upcoming events, contact the box office at (760) 202-2600.

The Canyons Lounge stages variety, comedy, and jazz performers nightly with no cover charge. Patrons can dance, relax in cabaret style seating, play video poker at the bar, or catch Monday Night Football and other sporting events on an extra large television screen. Call the entertainment hotline at (760) 321-2000 ext. 3499 to find out who is appearing currently.

BUS SERVICE

The casino provides free shuttle service in the Palm Desert area to and from major hotels and the airport. Call (760) 321-2000 about stops and times.

When you are ready to head for the next casino proceed eastward on Interstate 10 to Indio. Indio has long been an agricultural community, but its character is changing as development spreads in its direction. Indio bills itself as the "Date Capital of the World." The edible fruit of date palms is a treat known back to biblical times. If you are so inclined, you won't be disappointed if you do what millions of other travelers have done since 1924 and make a stop at Shields Date Farm on Highway 111 just west of Indio. Besides the taste delights of all varieties and forms of dates, including luscious date ice cream, you can enjoy the movie *The Romance and Sex Life of the Date*. It's free, instructional, amusing, and provides an opportunity to relax in their comfortable air-conditioned theater.

A new, small, start-up casino is located in Coachella. The Augustine Band of Cahuilla Mission Indians has 349 videos and slots and 10 table games. If you were at the Shield's Date Farm, continue east on Route 111 and turn right on Jackson Street in Indio. Proceed south to Avenue 54 and turn left, to the east, until crossing Van Buren. The Augustine Casino is located at the southeast corner. If you are going to the casino from I-10 in Indio take Monroe Road south for five miles to Avenue 54, then turn left two miles to Van Buren.

AUGUSTINE CASINO

Augustine Casino, 84-001 Avenue 54, Coachella, CA 92236
Owned by: Augustine Band of Cahuilla Mission Indians
Operated by: Augustine management & staff
Directions: East of Palm Springs on I-10, turn south in Indio on
    Monroe for 5 miles to Avenue 54, turn left 2 miles to Van Buren
Telephone: (760) 391-9500
Website: www.augustinecasino.com

Parking: **Valet:** Yes   **Indoor:** No   **Outdoor:** Yes
Bus service: No
Age for admittance: 21
Player's club: Yes, Augustine Gold
Nonsmoking area: No
Complimentary nonalcoholic drinks: Yes
Alcoholic beverages: No
Gift shop: No
Entertainment: No
Restaurants: Yes, 2: full-service and snack area
Casino size/gaming floor: 32,000/22,000 square feet

Table games: 10
Slots & video games: 349
Bingo: No
Offtrack betting: No
Poker room: No

Hotel: No
Golf course: No
Special attractions: Check their website for special events; many 1¢
    slots

SUMMARY 7

AUGUSTINE CASINO

T he Augustine Band of Cahuilla Mission Indians invited the public on July 18, 2002, to their new casino on the Augustine Reservation. The reservation, about a one-square mile tract, has been unoccupied for over 50 years until recently. It is located in an agricultural area of large palm groves, sprawling ranches, and new housing developments. The two-lane roads to the casino are straight as an arrow and slower than rural highways, but even so, the casino can be reached from the interstate in about 10 minutes.

TRIBAL AND CASINO HISTORY

For general history of the Cahuilla, see Chapter 1 in this book. The Augustine people are a band of the Desert Cahuilla Indians who occupied parts of the Mojave Desert from the Colorado River to the Coachella Valley area. The Augustine Reservation was officially established by executive order in 1891.

Presently the tribe has one adult member, Chairperson Maryann Martin. The original membership roll of 11 persons was approved by the Commissioner of Indian Affairs on April 13, 1956. The last surviving member, Roberta Ann Augustine, died on May 9, 1987, leaving three children and two grandchildren. Martin is one of her descendants and now has children of her own.

According to an EPA Waste Management Report, much of the land in this area of Coachella became a favorite dumping ground for residents, businesses, and farmers because of its remoteness and lack of population. Recently the reservation obtained a federal grant to clean up the area and accomplished the task, but they continued to fight an uphill battle trying to keep the property

Courtesy Augustine Casino

clear. With the casino and other activity now in the area, the problem is no longer an issue.

In 1996 Martin became the first member to establish residency on the Augustine Reservation since the 1950s. Not unexpectedly, Martin lacked the experience and resources to initiate the casino venture. How she happened to partner the tribe with an enterprising Las Vegas management company might be an interesting story, but unfortunately little information is available.

The public turnout for the opening was very large and casino operations seemed to function quite well. Under the direction of their management cadre of experienced professionals, it will run even more smoothly as local casino personnel gain more experience.

The Augustine Casino was newly built from the ground up on a flat parcel at the southeast corner of Van Buren and Avenue 54. The building is about 32,000 square feet in total size with about 75% of that for the gaming floor. Its outward appearance is like a typical industrial building, lacking significant architectural themes or adornments. However, as the landscaping (enhanced with soft lighting) takes hold, the casino will be an attractive beacon in this otherwise dull terrain.

The interior is well lighted and agreeably appointed with richly colored carpeting interspersed with areas of warm-colored ceramic tiles. The bar and dining area has rich wood walls accented with copper panels and is well furnished with comfortable seating. The large round bar separates the gaming floor from the dining area.

The overall effect, with its contemporary decorative theme, is of permanence and quality. For a start-up casino the management seems to have made prudent and economical choices. Chances are this casino will be successful as it caters to mostly local clientele. No doubt, in a few years it will be expanded, adding more features, gaming and glitz.

GAMES

With its 349 slots and 10 table games, the Augustine Casino is one of the smallest in southern California, but for its size it offers everything to attract the prospective customer base. It is easy to see the focus is on players with more modest pocketbooks as there is a large selection of videos games and slots of 5¢ and 25¢ denominations, even including many 1¢ machines. For the bigger spenders there is also a good mix of $1, $5, and $10 machines. Likewise Augustine is probably the only casino offering $1 blackjack. At the opening there was only one $1 table operating, the others being $5, but the casino plans to offer $1 blackjack at early morning sessions on a regular basis.

Among others, the 1¢ slots include Game King®, Texas Tea®, and The Frog Prince®. Several high payout name brands like $1,000,000 Pyramid™, and Regis' Cash Club™ played for 5¢ can deliver large jackpots. They also have many video poker games played in single and multiple hands for denominations from 5¢ to $1 and more.

In addition to the eight blackjack tables for play with stakes up to $500, they offer two tables for 3-card poker.

RESTAURANT

For quick snacks, desserts, and beverages, there is a walk-up snack bar adjoining the bar and restaurant. This keeps all food service in a compact area. Café 54 is the name of the full service restaurant that serves breakfast, lunch and dinner around the clock everyday. According to Food and Beverage Director Tim Hicks, their concept follows the old Las Vegas formula of attracting customers with excellent food at low prices. Full breakfast meals start from $4.95 while dinner entrées range from $6.95 to a prime beef New York strip steak dinner at $12.95. Prices bode well for hungry visitors to the Augustine Casino.

The next casino on the Jackpot Trail is Fantasy Springs just off the north side of I-10. If you are going there from the Augustine Casino, go back on Avenue 54 west to Jackson Street, then turn right to the north to Route 111 and follow it across the I-10 freeway. Route 111 becomes Golf Center Drive. Turn right at the first intersection past the freeway onto Indian Springs Parkway. Fantasy Springs Casino is just past the Holiday Express around the bend. If you are going there from I-10, take the Golf Center exit and cross over the freeway.

Courtesy Fantasy Springs Casino

John James, tribal chairman of Cabazon Band of Mission Indians, stands before a mural depicting a Cahuilla Indian clan gathered in the eastern Coachella Valley hundreds of years ago.

FANTASY SPRINGS CASINO

Fantasy Springs Casino, 84-245 Indio Springs Parkway, Indio, CA
  92203
Owned and operated by: Cabazon Band of Mission Indians
Directions: Interstate Highway 10, Golf Center exit, north side of
  freeway
Telephone: (800) 827-2946 toll free
Website: www.fantasyspringsresort.com

Parking: **Valet:** Yes   **Indoor:** No   **Outdoor:** Yes
Bus service: Yes, groups and tour
Age for admittance: 21
Player's club: Yes, Club Fantasy
Nonsmoking area: Yes
Complimentary nonalcoholic drinks: Yes
Alcoholic beverages: Yes
Gift shop: Yes
Entertainment: Yes, lounge and outdoor amphitheater
Restaurants: Yes, 3: fine dining, café, champagne brunch
Casino size/gaming floor: 265,000/85,000 square feet

Table games: 38
Slots & video games: 1,300
Bingo: Yes
Offtrack betting: Yes
Poker room: Yes

Hotel: No
Golf course: No
Special attractions: Cabazon Cultural Museum, 24-lane bowling
  center

SUMMARY 8

FANTASY SPRINGS CASINO

Fantasy Springs Casino is located on the reservation of the Cabazon Band of Mission Indians. The casino has been voted the Palm Springs area's "Best Overall Casino" for the past eight years by readers of the popular local daily newspaper, *The Desert Sun*. It's not just a gambling casino. Fantasy Springs is an all-around entertainment venue, open 24 hours a day, seven days a week. In addition to lounge entertainment and a 2,500-seat outdoor amphitheater, they have something unique among casinos, a 24-lane bowling center.

Fantasy Springs dominates a generous parcel of land with its modern architecture featuring a wide entryway. It is billed as the largest casino in the desert, having over 85,000 square feet of gaming area. Just outside the casino is an outdoor concert amphitheater, and within walking distance is a new cultural museum.

TRIBAL AND CASINO HISTORY

For early history of the Cahuilla, see Chapter 1 in this book. The Cabazon Band of Mission Indians was named after Chief Cabazon, their early leader who served as chief from the 1830s to the 1870s. Previously they were designated as a band of Desert Cahuilla Indians. There may be some confusion about the Cabazon Reservation name as it is also the name of the town 40 miles to the west, which is home to the Morongo Band of Mission Indians and the site for their casino.

When Anglo-Americans arrived in the 1840s they referred to all Native Americans as "Mission Indians" and the name has persisted in this case even

Courtesy Fantasy Springs Casino

though the Cabazon Band was never part of the mission system. The Cabazon and their forefathers, the Cahuilla, have a history that dates back thousands of years.

In recent times under the able leadership of Chairman John James, the Cabazon Band has established a successful gaming, entertainment, and environmental enterprise. The business is not just fun and games for this hardworking band. They have developed a state of the art recycling plant for disposing and making good use of old tires. First Nation Recovery, Inc. transforms tires into crumb rubber and scrap steel. The crumb rubber can be mixed with asphalt to produce a road paving material that lasts longer and absorbs noise to quiet traffic. The scrap steel is recycled for many uses. There is another plant for converting green waste into fuel. Called COLMAC, it processes green waste and uses the concentrated material to generate energy.

Gaming began with operation of a card room in 1980. Bingo was added in 1983. The Cabazon Band initiated the landmark case that ushered in full-fledged casino gambling in California. In *California v. Cabazon Band of Mission Indians, et al*, the U.S. Supreme Court found in favor of the Indians. Video gaming machines were then added in the early 1990s and video slot machines were installed in October 2000. At the same time a two-story addition was built to create 265,000 square foot of gaming and entertainment space.

Fantasy Springs Casino attracts more than one million visitors annually with options of bingo (including video bingo that can be played in English or Spanish), blackjack, poker and other card games, 1,300 slot machines, and off-track betting. Recreational and competitive bowling is available for all members of the family. The casino hosts frequent promotions offering guests a chance to win a car, a vacation, cash, and other major prizes.

Fantasy Springs Casino's new walk-in gift shop is called Painted Canyon Collectibles. It reflects an exciting new direction in its theme and merchandise. The shop is a large inviting space located near the new rear entrance to the casino. Painted Canyon Collectibles carries clothing and souvenir items emblazoned with the Cabazon Band of Mission Indians and Fantasy Springs Casino logos. More impressive is a large selection of Native American-made items including pottery, carvings, dreamcatchers, mandellas, books, cards, and music.

GAMES

Fantasy Springs Casino claims to have the most diverse mix of Las Vegas style slot machines in all of California. In total, Fantasy Springs has more than 1,300 of the most entertaining and exciting machines presently available from established gaming suppliers. Some of the new machines, which accept a variety of denominations, offer multiple games. Certain machines are networked with progressive nationwide jackpots that pay off as high as $15 million. Some slot games feature video screens while others employ the traditional spinning reels.

For table games, there is something for everyone. The blackjack pit has 13 new tables including Las Vegas style blackjack, Caribbean Stud®, Let It Ride®, progressive blackjack, 3-card poker, and mini-baccarat.

The new nonsmoking poker room boasts nine poker tables offering a variety of games with low to high ranging limits including: Texas Hold'Em, Omaha hi-lo, 7-card stud, and 8 or better. Poker tournaments are played daily. Poker lessons are given every Tuesday at 4 p.m. For more information about Fantasy Springs' poker or table games, call (800) 827-2946.

Bingo is played seven days per week at Fantasy Springs Casino, with a wide variety of exciting sessions. There are two main sessions daily, and players can enjoy bingo for as little as $1 during daily matinee sessions. On weekends (Friday, Saturday and Sunday), the main session regular games pay $600 or $1,199.

Players may avail themselves of the latest and most popular electronic bingo machines on the market today, both portables and fixed terminal. Monday through Thursday the buy-in is $10 for the main session. Special promotional nights are featured each month where players win up to $1,000 and 90 days of free bingo. Club Fantasy members play bingo free on their birthdays.

Offtrack betting coverage is complete with all major racetracks, all major races, and all California racetracks, including California fairs, night racing, quarter horse, and harness racing. The Triple Crown Room has a capacity of 562, with the main room seating 300 and the VIP Room seating 50 with 11 tables.

Program racing forms, digests, tip sheets and newspapers are available for purchase. The 9 by 12-foot TV projection screen plus another 39 large TV sets, make viewing convenient and exciting.

For the further convenience of offtrack betting players, there are eight automatic betting machines, six teller windows, and a voucher machine. Add to this the VIP Room, open bar, food service, coffee and popcorn all day long, and you have one of the best offtrack betting facilities to be found. The facility is nonsmoking and has a handy smoking patio.

Sign up for Club Fantasy as soon as you enter the casino to take advantage of the many free benefits. Slot machines keep track of your points every time you play. The more you play the more you earn. You can collect points at the table games too; just give your card to the casino attendant. Points are convertible to cash and merchandise. Members receive complimentary rewards such as invitations to member only events and tournaments, exclusive offers, discount mailers, tickets for headliner entertainment, and preferred seating for world-class boxing. Club members may also receive discounts at the gift shop, Fantasy Lanes, bingo, and restaurants, plus a free subscription to the *Club Fantasy Newsletter*.

RESTAURANTS

For great atmosphere and food the critically acclaimed Players Fine Dining is open nightly for dinner. It is considered one of the finest in the desert. The newly renovated restaurant is open nightly for dinner and features award-winning cuisine, a romantic ambience, and boasts a loyal clientele who know a good thing when they find it. An early bird menu is available certain days. Dining hours vary. Call for hours and reservations at (800) 827-2946.

The Fantasy Bar & Grille is a comfortable spot that serves an extensive menu ranging from ham and eggs, steaks, pasta and seafood, to eclectic salads and old-time dessert favorites. The Fantasy Bar & Grille is open 24 hours a day, seven days a week.

A delicious Sunday Champagne Brunch is served in the Fantasy Lounge between 10 a.m. and 2 p.m. for $14.95 per person. Brunch includes a custom omelet station, carving stations, a dessert island and unlimited champagne. A live combo playing jazz music sets the mood for a relaxing dining experience. No reservations are required.

ENTERTAINMENT

Regular weekly shows in Fantasy Lounge include everything from country western to upbeat Latino music. During the summer of 2002, the 5,000-seat outdoor Under the Stars Amphitheater played host to the Beach Boys and other major entertainment acts. Previous entertainers who have performed there include LeAnn Rimes, The Moody Blues, Faith Hill, Bill Cosby, Kenny Rogers, and Trisha Yearwood.

BUS SERVICE

For information about tour buses or group sales, call (800) 827-2946, ext. 3251 for tour buses, and ext. 3038 for group sales.

Courtesy Fantasy Springs Casino

CABAZON CULTURAL MUSEUM

For 20 years members of the Cabazon Band dreamed of having a permanent home for their tribal artifacts and a place to teach, display, and maintain all elements of their culture. This dream became a reality in April 2002 when they opened the Cabazon Cultural Museum, just across the street from the Fantasy Springs Casino. The exhibits are interesting and well designed to acquaint visitors with the rich heritage of the Desert Cahuilla Indians. The museum is just a short walk from the casino and well worth visiting, especially by the kids and grandkids. The Cabazon Band has a saying, "Tax'islu E'lis," meaning to look forward, look back. Taking a look back in history gives us a better understanding of the present and helps us to look into the future with greater insight.

BOWLING CENTER

The Fantasy Lanes Family Bowling Center, is conveniently connected to Fantasy Springs Casino. This state of the art 24-lane bowling center has a cocktail lounge, snack bar and pro shop. The bowling balls are spectacular with glowing lights and laser beams in a mix of colors. The lanes are high-tech. Children and beginners will love using the programmable bumpers that prevent gutter balls. Tournaments and league bowling is available for various age groups. Weekends and holidays bring special events, tournaments, and prizes. The center offers laser bowling to music Friday and Saturday nights from 9:30 p.m. until 2 a.m. Call Fantasy Lanes for more information at (800) 827-2946, extension 3011.

Courtesy Fantasy Springs Casino

Fantasy Springs bowling alley

The next destination along the Desert Branch is Trump 29 Casino, only a few miles away. Take the I-10 east about a half-mile to the Dillon Road exit.

TRUMP 29 CASINO

Trump 29 Casino, 46-200 Harrison Place, Coachella, CA 92236
Owned by: Twentynine Palms Enterprises Corporation, a wholly
  owned enterprise of the Twentynine Palms Band of Mission
  Indians
Operated by: Trump Hotels and Casino Resorts, Inc.
Directions: Interstate Highway 10, east of Indio, Dillon Road exit
Telephone: (866) TRUMP 29 (878-6729) toll free
Website: www.trump29.com

Parking: **Valet:** Yes   **Indoor:** No   **Outdoor:** Yes
Bus service: Yes, local and tour
Age for admittance: 21 to gamble; under 21 must be escorted
Player's club: Yes, Chairman's Club, Gold and Platinum
Nonsmoking area: Yes
Complimentary nonalcoholic drinks: Yes
Alcoholic beverages: Yes
Gift shop: Yes
Entertainment: Yes, lounge, 2,300-seat theater showroom
Restaurants: Yes, 6: gourmet dining, café & buffet, Asian, pizza, deli,
  McDonald's
Casino size/gaming floor: 200,000/100,000 square feet

Table games: 35
Slots & video games: 2,000
Bingo: No
Offtrack betting: No
Poker room: No

Hotel: No
Golf course: No
Special attractions: Check the website for special events and headline
  entertainment.

SUMMARY 9

TRUMP 29 CASINO

In April 2002, Donald Trump and the Twentynine Palms Band of Mission Indians formally opened the Trump 29 Casino in Coachella as the successor to Spotlight 29 Casino. This stylish $60 million casino completed phase one of an ongoing program, which according to its developers, will "bring the best in modern gambling and entertainment to the desert." Its location, just off the Dillon Road exit from Interstate Highway 10, is one of the easiest to reach.

TRIBAL AND CASINO HISTORY

For early tribal history of the Chemehuevi, see Chapter 1 in this book. Members of the Twentynine Palms Band of Mission Indians are descendants of the Chemehuevi Indians who migrated from the Colorado River and settled into remote areas of the Mojave Desert in the mid-1860s. The band was named after the region around the oasis of Twentynine Palms where they settled around 1867. The area was then known as the Oasis of Mara and is presently the city of Twentynine Palms.

Later, after the arrival of the white man, the tribe members sought employment on ranches and farms in Banning and the Coachella Valley. They also worked in mines, which were scattered through the region.

An executive order signed by President Grover Cleveland in 1895 designated 160 acres of tribal lands at Twentynine Palms as reservation land. In 1910, the government added 640 acres to the Cabazon Reservation in Indio for

Courtesy Trump 29 Casino

joint occupation by Cahuilla and Chemehuevi tribes. In 1974 Congress split the Cabazon Reservation, providing 240 acres exclusively for the Twentynine Palms Band. The casino is located on a portion of this land.

The Twentynine Palms Band is intent on insuring that Indians and non-Indians have the opportunity to share the remaining vestiges of Indian culture left in the nearby area, and they have taken measures to protect cultural resources. The band is a member of the Native American Land Conservancy (NALC), which recently purchased 2,500 acres in the Old Woman Mountains containing a shaman's cave with paintings made by Indians hundreds of years ago.

Dean Mike is presently the Chairman of the Twentynine Palms Band. Mike's grandfather was William Mike, who led the tribe at the Twentynine Palms Reservation for many years. In order to earn much needed cash, William took his people to the Gilman Ranch in Banning for work every summer. In 1909, most of the Chemehuevi from Twentynine Palms moved to the Morongo Reservation before their eventual relocation to the Cabazon Reservation. The Mike family first moved to the Torres Martinez Reservation and later settled in Palm Springs. As an adult, Dean moved to the state of Washington where he worked as a fisheries biologist technician with the Lummi Tribe. He returned to Coachella in 1994 to help develop the Spotlight 29 Casino in Coachella.

In the early 1990s, the tribe considered many business proposals including gaming. After several years of negotiations and federal review, the tribe developed the Spotlight 29 Casino. Although they owned Spotlight 29 Casino, the tribe lacked the experience and manpower to operate a modern casino. Originally the tribe worked with two management companies, but in 2000 they entered into a management agreement with Trump Hotels and Casino Resorts, Inc., the management firm of renowned real estate mogul Donald Trump. The name of the casino was changed to Trump 29 to fully reflect the involvement of the Trump organization.

The casino's architectural style is clean and modern, yet with a retro look. The 200,000 square foot property reflects the influence of Hollywood on Palm Springs, circa 1950. It has a subtle touch of glamour with a splash of desert color accented in wood, stone, glass, and stainless steel.

Technifex, an entertainment technology company, created special visual effects to further intrigue patrons. Realistic roaring flames called "FauxFire" are created on a 60-foot casino wall. The simulated fire is generated by a high-pressure steam flow illuminated with specialty lighting. A computer control system varies the flame's height and intensity throughout the day to add realism to the effect.

It is interesting to note that the first phase plan included a special lounge called The Platinum Club, for "frequent players." This private, posh, and sophisticated hideaway, where preferred customers can relax and enjoy beverages and snacks, is located on the second floor. Special attention accorded to important customers is apparently a trademark of the Trump organization.

Mark A. Brown, President and CEO of Trump Hotels and Casino Resorts, Inc., was previously president and COO of Trump Taj Mahal and Trump Marina. In his new capacity, Brown oversees all gaming operations for the Trump organization. Though just 40 years old, Mark has over 20 years experience in the gaming business in New Jersey, where he earned his reputation as "the man people like to work for." Mark Lefever, General Manager of Trump 29, has a strong financial background and many years in the casino business in Las Vegas and New Jersey. He is a CPA and member of the American Institute of Certified Public Accountants. Obviously, the tribal members and Donald Trump want to know precisely where the money is flowing.

GAMES

Prior to the phase two expansion, the casino operated 1,300 slots of the typical varieties and 15 table games featuring blackjack, Pai Gow, plus the traditional and specialty poker games. Post phase two the casino has 2,000 slots, the maximum number allowed by law, and a total of 35 table games to put them on par with the largest Indian casinos in California.

Bingo enthusiasts and those who frequent offtrack betting parlors will not find these options at Trump 29, but that should not deter them from enjoying the many other features and excitement of this first-rate casino.

The Chairman's Club is Trump 29's answer to player's clubs. Like others, it is a way to accumulate points as you play. Newcomers start with the gold card, which makes them immediately eligible for special invitations, bonus point days, discounts and many other benefits. Consistent and frequent players who achieve a certain level of play in a three-month period are issued a platinum player's card, which gives them extra special benefits for the next quarter. The most visible and impressive is membership to the Platinum Lounge off the Blue Bar and Lounge.

RESTAURANTS

Just inside the main entrance to the right is the open and spacious 200-seat Café Capitata. This 24-hour eatery offers full service table meals and buffet service under an umbrella of attractive mood-setting palm trees.

Phase two opened in September 2002. Major new additions include an upscale 140-seat restaurant called the Rattlesnake Club. It features the cuisine of chef/entrepreneur Jimmy Schmidt, who opened the first Rattlesnake Club in Denver in 1988. He followed that success with another top award winning Rattlesnake Club in Detroit. Schmidt is an active author and columnist well known in select cooking circles and increasingly admired by his many fans since publishing three popular cookbooks.

For the more casual diner, phase two brings favorites to suit all tastes: City Wok's Asian dishes, a deli, pizza shop, and for the inveterate fast-food junkies, McDonald's.

ENTERTAINMENT

Blue is described as a red-hot cool lounge, where music and entertainment never stop. If the description seems incongruous, you will have to see it yourself and make your own assessment. From its second tier perch customers can relax and view the entire casino floor including the "fiery" display while enjoying their favorite cocktail.

The most spectacular addition in phase two is the 2,300-seat indoor theater, touted as the largest and finest in the desert. No doubt the influence and experience of Trump Hotels and Casino Resorts, Inc. will attract top name entertainers to wow the winter season Palm Springs crowd and local casino goers. The Trump organization has not disclosed plans for full-scale resort development of a hotel, golf course, or other amenities. For the present they seem to be focusing on the combination of first-rate casino action and the best entertainment in the area to attract customers.

Trump 29 is the last stop of the closely aggregated casinos of the Desert Branch. To reach the last casino, Havasu Landing Resort and Casino on the Colorado River, there are some wide stretches of desert to cross.

The Havasu Landing Casino is small, and there's little else on the California side of the Colorado River unless you are a camper or RV traveler. However, another justification for making the lengthy trip across the desert is to visit Lake Havasu City, which is across the river/lake on the Arizona side. Lake Havasu City is a tourist mecca, especially for those who enjoy water sports. If you approach Havasu Landing Casino from the California side, however, you cannot drive across at that point to Lake Havasu City. There is only a passenger ferry connection. It also should be noted for our travelers on the Jackpot Trail that the California route to Havasu Landing is very desolate, whereas the route we suggest to Lake Havasu City is far more interesting and scenic.

A special word is offered to RV travelers and campers. You may wish to stay at Havasu Landing, as they have excellent facilities. However, we suggest you make reservations, especially in peak seasons. Call (800) 307-3610.

Whichever route you choose, take I-10 east to Desert Center, then go north on SR 177 to where it intersects SR 62. Continue east on SR 62 to Vidal Junction. This intersection with U.S. Highway 95 consists of a small store and gas station and is the only place within many miles for supplies. If you wish to stay on the California side of the Colorado, go north on U.S. 95 to Havasu Lake Road, then turn east. For the scenic route and to reach Lake Havasu City, stay on SR 62 east. It's about 15 miles to Parker Dam, on top of which the road crosses the Colorado into Arizona.

Leaving the dam, the road heads south about a mile before intersecting Route 95. Take a sharp turn to the left and head north on Route 95 to Lake Havasu City, which is about 25 miles away.

To get to the Havasu Landing Resort and Casino from Lake Havasu City, turn west onto McCollough Road and cross the famous London Bridge. Immediately after crossing the bridge turn right into the parking lot. This is the place to leave your car while you make the excursion to the casino. Look for stairways that go to the water level. You will see the sign for the casino ferry. It leaves about every hour on the half hour and returns on the hour. It takes about 25 minutes to cross the lake. The cost is $2 per person, round trip.

There are dozens of hotels, motels, and resorts, all types of shops and restaurants, and a wide variety of establishments offering water sports in Lake Havasu City. Once you have come this far on the Desert Branch of the Jackpot Trail, you should stop, relax, and enjoy yourself.

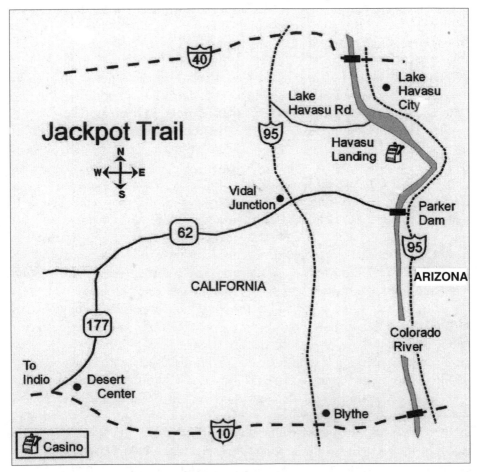

Map 7. Desert Branch — East Sector

HAVASU LANDING RESORT AND CASINO

Havasu Landing Resort and Casino, 1 Main Street, Havasu Lake, CA
   92363
Owned and operated by: Chemehuevi Indian Tribe
Directions: California route, I-10 east to Desert Center, north on
   SR 177 to SR 62 east to Vidal Junction, take U.S. Highway 95
   north to Havasu Lake Road; Arizona route, from Vidal Junction
   stay on SR 62 across Parker Dam, take U.S. Highway 95 north to
   Lake Havasu City
Telephone: (800) 307-3610 toll free
Website: www.havasulanding.com

Parking: **Valet:** Yes   **Indoor:** Yes   **Outdoor:** Yes
Bus service: No
Age for admittance: 21
Player's club: No
Nonsmoking area: No
Complimentary nonalcoholic drinks: No
Alcoholic beverages: Yes
Gift shop: No **Entertainment:** No
Restaurants: Yes, 1: full-service
Casino size/gaming floor: 11,000/6,000 square feet

Table games: 5
Slots & video games: 220
Bingo: No
Offtrack betting: No
Poker room: No

Hotel: No
Golf course: No
Special attractions: Near Lake Havasu City; RV park, camp-
   grounds, water recreational sports, landing strip and tie-downs for
   small jets and aircraft nearby, marina, and mobile home park

SUMMARY 10

HAVASU LANDING RESORT AND CASINO

The Havasu Landing Resort and Casino, nestled on the shoreline of the Colorado River's Lake Havasu is small, but it has some unusual features. It can be reached either by land, air, or water. It has many options for RV travelers and campers, not the least of which is water recreation. And here's an intriguing thought — if you really enjoy the place, you can live there in your own mobile home. Though located in a remote section of the Mojave Desert with little of California civilization nearby, it is part of the large booming resort center of Lake Havasu City just across the river in Arizona.

Without an RV or equipment for camping out, there is only a small 10-room motel nearby on the California side for overnight sojourners. The next nearest lodgings in California are at Needles, more than 60 miles away. It is yet a longer road trip finding lodging across the river in Lake Havasu City. Visitors driving to the casino on the California side should plan ahead.

TRIBAL AND CASINO HISTORY

For the early history of the Chemehuevi, see Chapter 1 in this book. In the late 1980s the Chemehuevi made a commitment to develop land abutting the Colorado River at Lake Havasu as a source of income. What started as an RV park has now taken on much greater importance since gaming was introduced in the 1990s. Casino operations are small compared to most Indian casinos, but

Courtesy Havasu Landing Resort and Casino

they have added significantly to the resort's attraction and profitability. The business enterprises are under the direction of Tribal Leader Tito Smith.

The main building of the property includes about 6,000 square feet of gaming floor. Overall it has about 11,000 square feet, with the restaurant and lounge occupying the majority of the remaining space. A $5.5 million expansion and refurbishment project was completed in July 2002 and long-range plans call for a much larger casino with many new features. Because of its small size, there is no provision for a nonsmoking section at present.

The building sits right on the shore, so close that it extends over the water. If the height of Lake Havasu were not regulated by Parker Dam to the south, the casino could conceivably flood at times. The proximity of the casino to the lake is an attribute that adds a certain character and charm to the place.

A boat brings patrons from Lake Havasu City to a dock on the south side of the casino. The dock is connected by a short walkway to the casino entrance. The boat schedule from the London Bridge at Lake Havasu City to the casino is from 7 a.m. to 12:30 a.m. with departures every hour. The service extends to about 2:30 a.m. on Friday and Saturday.

GAMES

For the available 220 slots and video games, there is a good mix of popular titles, video poker, and progressives, with most being 5¢ to $1 denominations.

Courtesy Havasu Landing Resort and Casino

Playing the slot machines at the river casino

Table games, five in total, are mostly blackjack with the exception of one 3-card poker table. Tables are in operation Wednesday through Sunday from 3 p.m. until "late" according to the management. As more staff members are hired the hours will be extended to seven days a week, with morning and later evening hours. The casino slots and video games are available every day starting at 9:30 a.m. The casino closes at 12:30 a.m. Sunday through Thursday, and 2:30 a.m. Friday and Saturday.

RESTAURANT

The Landing Resort Restaurant provides table service for basic American cuisine. The view of Lake Havasu from the restaurant provides an inviting touch. The restaurant opens at 9:30 a.m. every day. It closes at 9 p.m. Sunday through Thursday and 11 p.m. Friday and Saturday.

RESORT FEATURES

This desert setting on expansive Lake Havasu has a great deal of appeal to campers for its peacefulness, beauty, and outdoor recreational opportunities. Those who are properly equipped will find Havasu Landing an excellent base of operations. For those who are looking for special equipment for water excitement, they can widen their scope to the more populous Lake Havasu City. The resort area has a market, deli and gas station. The RV park and campground has a laundromat, showers, storage and other amenities. Overnight hookups for a single night are $22 dollars and somewhat higher for holidays. The overnight camping fee is $10.

Recreational activities include water skiing, boating, swimming, fishing, hunting, jet skiing, windsurfing, sightseeing and seasonal events in the area.

Those with small jets and planes can fly in for lunch or fun and games. Pilots can contact the beacon at Unicom 122.9. The airstrip is one mile long and 75 feet wide. Twenty tie-downs are available and there are no landing fees. The casino provides free shuttle transportation.

The marina is in a protected cove near the casino. It has boat slips and three boat ramps. The marina provides launch and retrieval service, the cheapest gas on the river, and convenient access to the general store.

In addition to catering to the needs and interests of transient visitors, Havasu Landing Resort and Casino offers long-term land leases in one of the four mobile home parks for those who wish to establish a more permanent base of operations at this diversified recreational location. There are a total of 430 leased lots. They have more lots available with great views of Lake Havasu. A new mobile home park with a marina is in the planning stages, and refurbishment and expansion of the current RV park and campground is underway.

CHAPTER 7
UPLAND BRANCH
RIVERSIDE COUNTY

From Interstate 10 on the western end of the Desert Branch, go south on SR 79 in Beaumont. This is a beautiful drive all the way from Beaumont to your first stop, the Soboba Casino. Continue through the foothills on the new divided highway until you reach the San Jacinto River basin. Turn east on Gilman Springs Road from SR 79. Just past the Golden Era Golf Course is a turn to the left to Soboba Road. Follow this a few miles to the casino.

The small casino at Soboba is a friendly place to visit and one where you will find your favorite games. The Soboba Band of the Luiseño Indians extends their warm Indian greeting "Miiyu," welcome. If you are ready for a meal at this time, try the Soboba Steakhouse for great food at reasonable prices.

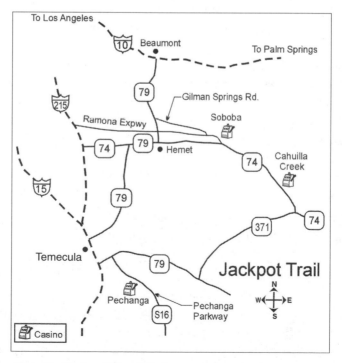

Map 8. Upland Branch

SOBOBA CASINO

Soboba Casino, 23333 Soboba Road, San Jacinto, CA 92581
Owned and operated by: Soboba Band of Luiseño Indians
Directions: From I-10 toward Palm Springs, south on SR 79 in
    Beaumont, turn east on Gilman Springs Road; after the Golden Era
    Golf Course, turn to the left onto Soboba Road
Telephone: (866) 4-SOBOBA (476-2622) or (888) 772-7626 toll free
Website: www.soboba.com

Parking: **Valet:** Yes   **Indoor:** No   **Outdoor:** Yes
Bus service: No
Age for admittance: 21
Player's club: No
Nonsmoking area: No
Complimentary nonalcoholic drinks: Yes
Alcoholic beverages: Yes
Gift shop: Yes
Entertainment: Yes, lounge, outdoor arena
Restaurants: Yes, 3: steakhouse, café, oriental
Casino size/gaming floor: 80,000/60,000 square feet

Table games: 21
Slots & video games: 2,000
Bingo: Yes
Offtrack betting: No
Poker room: No

Hotel: No
Golf course: No
Special attractions: Call or check the website for casino promotions,
    special events, and the outdoor concert schedule.

SUMMARY 11

SOBOBA CASINO

T he Soboba Casino, owned and operated by the Soboba Band of Luiseño Indians, is on the edge of the city of San Jacinto north of Hemet on the slopes of the San Jacinto Mountains. The Soboba Reservation spreads over the southern slopes of this mountain mass, which shapes the Palm Springs basin and the San Jacinto River plain. It occupies a complex of large tent structures having modest exterior architectural features.

TRIBAL AND CASINO HISTORY

For the early history of the Cahuilla and Luiseño, see Chapter 1 in this book. The original 5,000-acre reservation was established by executive order in 1883. Since that time the reservation has grown to about 7,000 acres. The first residents were Indians of the Cahuilla tribe. Later, as Indians were indiscriminately relocated throughout southern California, many of the Luiseño moved onto the reservation and became the dominant group.

As early as 1880, southern California Indian observers like Helen Hunt Jackson, author of *Ramona* and *A Century of Dishonor*, reported that the Soboba were diligent and industrious people. They have engaged in extensive farming over the years on the San Jacinto River plain, growing crops of tomatoes, pumpkins, and squash. More recently their commercial citrus groves have produced high quality fruit for export to Japan. The riverbed has also been a rich resource for sand and gravel, which is sold for construction purposes.

The Soboba now have a population of 800 members, with about half living on the reservation today in scattered houses. The tribal buildings include an old

Courtesy Soboba Casino

chapel and cemetery, new tribal offices, an education center, a medical clinic, and a sports complex. The most notable structure now on the Soboba Reservation is the casino. The tribal chairman is Robert J. Salgado.

The first casino was erected in 1998. After three expansions the tent-type casino structure is now close to 80,000 square feet. The building includes about 60,000 square feet of gaming floor, a steakhouse, café, oriental restaurant, lounge, and gift shop. The gift shop, located near the front entrance, has a good assortment of Soboba logo caps, T-shirts and other souvenirs.

GAMES

Players will find a wide assortment of the latest and most popular slots and video games among the full complement of 2,000 machines clustered about the gaming floor. Name brand machines such as Elvira®, Hollywood Squares®, Scrabble®, Wheel of Fortune®, and $1,000,000 Pyramid™, a wide variety of reel type slots including Blazing 7s®, X-Factor™, and Stampede®, and many progressive jackpot games are clustered about the gaming floor. The casino also offers a new penny slot area called Land O'Lincoln. For the video poker players there are 200 machines of single-hand, up to 50 hands per screen. Machine denominations are from 5¢ to $5 with a high percentage of 5¢ and 25¢ machines. In recent months Soboba slot players have hit jackpots of $47,000 with total jackpots of well over $1 million.

They also have the latest and hottest video blackjack for five players seated at a table facing a video screen dealer. This game is played exactly like the table counterpart with the same odds of winning. Another unusual game is Royal Derby®, a simulated horse race on video.

The casino has 21 table games of which 15 are devoted to blackjack, which is played with six deck shoes and stakes of $5 to $500. Specialty table games of Pai Gow poker, Let It Ride®, 3-card poker, mini-baccarat, and the more traditional poker games of 7-card stud, Omaha, and Texas Hold'Em are open for play 24 hours a day.

A player's club, called Club Soboba, has recently been introduced. Club members earn points for play to be redeemed for food, merchandise, and event tickets.

RESTAURANTS

Soboba offers diners a choice of three distinctive restaurants to satisfy everyone from the gourmet to the "eat on the run" person. For a sit-down dining experience, the Soboba Steakhouse is recommended. This comfortable restaurant serves prime rib, steaks, pastas, and much more. The restaurant also serves breakfast and lunch throughout the day. For more contemporary tastes and a lighter fare, there is the Café Soboba that offers a menu of burgers, hot and cold sandwiches, and a variety of snacks and drinks. The café is open 24 hours, seven

Courtesy Soboba Casino

Interior of Soboba Casino

days a week. For those looking for something to perk up their taste buds, the Spicy Sushi service may do the trick. The oriental specialties of sushi, teriyaki bowls, and other specialties are individually prepared to bring diners the exotic flavors of Asian dishes. Spicy Sushi is open Sunday through Thursday from 11 a.m. to 10 p.m. and from 11 a.m. to 2 a.m. Friday and Saturday. A lunch buffet is served everyday in the lounge area for $6.95, and a dinner buffet is served in the same area on Wednesday for $9.95 and on Thursday for $11.95.

ENTERTAINMENT

There is a limited amount of live entertainment in the vicinity of San Jacinto and Hemet. This provides the Soboba Casino an added incentive to bring more enjoyment to its customers and area residents on a year-round basis. The evening outdoor summer concert series brings top name musical groups such as Lynard Skynard, Dwight Yoakam, and the Beach Boys. There are also exciting ring matches such as King of the Cage and Battle of the Badges. The arena can seat up to 10,000, with all seats having a great view of the action. Rodeos and other events are also scheduled.

Inside the casino, the Sports Lounge also offers live entertainment with program variations nightly, such as country, Mexican, Top 40 disc jockey, swing band, and karaoke.

When you leave the casino, cross over the San Jacinto riverbed and take Main Street into the quaint town of San Jacinto. A trip down Main Street is a flashback in time to the 1920s and 1930s. If you are older, nostalgia will reign as you view the stores and residences of that period. As you move down Main

Street, look for the signs for SR 79, and turn left (south). After about a mile, SR 79 turns sharply to the right (west) onto Florida Street in Hemet.

If you have time before you leave Hemet, and if it is April, you might want to attend the Ramona Pageant. This outdoor spectacular enacts the story of *Ramona* written by Indian sympathizer Helen Hunt Jackson. Jackson based the story on the real and tragic events of local Indians. For information about the annual event, call the pageant office at (909) 658-3114.

Continue through Hemet several miles, and be watchful for the intersection where SR 79 turns again to the south toward Winchester. After passing through Winchester, which isn't much more than an intersection with a few stores, watch for the Domenigoni Valley Reservoir on the east side of the highway. This $2 billion recently completed reservoir, fed from the Colorado River, is one of the largest water projects of the past one 100 years. It covers over 18,000 acres at depths up to 250 feet, providing enough water to supply the needs of 13 million people.

Visit the public viewing area, just to the east of the highway. The reservoir's vast expanse of water and three earthen dams are a sight worth stopping to see. You will also find information about important discoveries of fossils, huge mastodons, giant ground sloths, camels, lions and other extinct animals that were uncovered while digging for the dams. These fossils date from the Pleistocene epoch, from two million years to 10,000 years ago when Indians first began to inhabit the area.

As you continue on SR 79, you will pass through the gentle plains of French Valley and into the spreading development of Temecula, where growth has been rampant in recent years. If you have need for shopping, this is the best place for it on the Upland Branch.

At Interstate 15, turn south toward San Diego and be prepared to turn off again at the second exit, which is the continuation of SR 79. Take the left hand turn, under the freeway, and proceed eastward about a half mile to Pechanga Parkway. Turn right and in a few minutes you will be at the Pechanga Resort and Casino, one of California's most spectacular new casinos.

Temecula has other worthy attractions for visitors. The "Old Town" area, which is on the west side of I-15, is a quaint place to spend time strolling through the western style façaded shops, which include numerous restaurants, gift and antique shops. The Temecula Valley is also southern California's premier wine country with more than a dozen wineries within a short drive from Pechanga. For travelers who enjoy fine wines and are not especially familiar with the wineries of the Temecula Valley area, you will be impressed with their high quality, good prices, and attractive tasting rooms.

PECHANGA RESORT AND CASINO

Pechanga Resort and Casino, 45000 Pechanga Parkway, Temecula,
CA 92592
Owned and operated by: Pechanga Band of Luiseño Indians
Directions: From I-15 in Temecula take SR 79 east to Pechanga
Parkway, turn right, the casino is two miles ahead on the right
Telephone: (888) 732-4264 toll free
Website: www.pechanga.com

Parking: **Valet:** Yes   **Indoor:** Yes   **Outdoor:** Yes
Bus service: Yes, special tour arrangements only
Age for admittance: 21
Player's club: Yes, Player Rewards Club
Nonsmoking area: Yes
Complimentary nonalcoholic drinks: Yes
Alcoholic beverages: Yes
Gift shop: Yes, 2
Entertainment: Yes, 4 lounges and a 1,200-seat showroom
Restaurants: Yes, 6: steakhouse, seafood, Italian, buffet, café, Asian
Casino size/gaming floor: 125,000/80,000 square feet

Table games: 63
Slots & video games: 2,000
Bingo: Yes
Offtrack betting: No
Poker room: Yes

Hotel: Yes, 522 rooms and suites, swimming pool, convention facilities
Golf course: No
Special attractions: Performing arts theatre, RV park, gas station,
mini-mart, car wash; near Old Town Temecula

SUMMARY 12

PECHANGA RESORT AND CASINO

The new Pechanga Resort and Casino in Temecula, which opened June 23, 2002, is one of the most developed Indian gaming enterprises in California. Although Pechanga (pronounced pe-chän-guh) will not have a golf course for a few years, there are two excellent courses within a five-minute drive, Redhawk and Temecula Creek.

The Pechanga Resort and Casino features a modern resort hotel and convention center with a 125,000 square foot casino. It has one of the best designed performing arts theaters in southern California, a recreational vehicle park, and an auto service center and mart, all within a five minute drive from Interstate 15.

TRIBAL AND CASINO HISTORY

For general history of the Luiseño, see Chapter 1 in this book. The Pechanga Band of Luiseño Indians trace their origins in the Temecula Valley to over 10,000 years ago, as documented by archaeological artifacts. They are a band of the Luiseño tribe that occupied large areas of San Diego and Riverside Counties.

In 1875 a group of Temecula Valley ranchers petitioned the District Court of San Francisco and were granted a decree of ownership to the land, which entitled them to evict the Indian people who occupied much of the Temecula

Courtesy Pechanga Resort and Casino

Valley, from near their present location to north and east of Old Town Temecula.

The sheriff of San Diego County led a posse that forcibly removed the Indians and dumped them, along with whatever possessions they could carry or cart, to the hills south of the valley. This is the land the Pechanga still occupy. It is about two miles east of I-15 and much of it can be seen if coming north on the freeway, just beyond the immigration control checkpoint.

These industrious Indians were, and are, a proud people with a strong spirit. Their ancestors moved to a small, secluded area where they rebuilt their village and lives. This place was called *Pechaa'ang*, named after a spring that provided fresh water since ancient times. Thus they became known as the Pechanga Band of the Luiseño Indian tribe — people who live at Pechaa'ang.

In a fortuitous twist of fate for the Pechanga, it turned out that the new land they occupied was the most fertile in the valley. White ranchers were soon envious of the bountiful crops being raised by the Indians and were likely coveting this area. However, in 1882 an executive order by the President of the United States, though stridently opposed by the California Legislature, established Pechanga as a reservation. Additional acreage was added over the years to bring the current total to about 4,500 acres.

Over the years they made the most of their holdings and strove to improve their position through a strong community of tribal members. In recent generations tribal members have used all educational means available to improve their lot. Now, many members hold college degrees. They have distinguished themselves even beyond the Indian communities and are the core of tribal leadership.

For example, Tribal Chairman Mark Macarro, a graduate of the University of California at Santa Barbara, is known throughout California as spokesman for the Proposition 5 initiative, the Indian Self-Reliance Act. Macarro is on several gaming governing boards in the state and nationally and is the only Indian member of Governor Gray Davis' California Workforce Investment Act Board.

In 1994 the band's general membership created the Pechanga Development Corporation (PDC) to focus efforts on economic development. The advent of enabling legislation for gaming in the early 1990s provided new prospects. PDC engaged in planning and development that led to the first gaming facility, which opened in July 1995. With little fanfare or publicity, Pechanga soon attracted many customers, and their facility grew rapidly as revenues increased.

Now after seven years, the Pechanga Band has moved from single-story temporary structures to the luxurious surroundings of a modern $260 million casino, resort, and hotel complex. Anthony Miranda, president of the PDC, takes pride in saying that what they have accomplished is the collective result of the efforts of all tribal members during the past decade. Under the guidance of the PDC, the Pechanga Indians have steadily advanced to become a major destination gaming resort location. They have hired top notch industry talent to provide the needed expertise, but management is under direct control of tribal members.

The exterior and interior architecture and décor of the casino, resort, and hotel complex is clean and straightforward, with a hint of elegance in its design and features. There has been no attempt to create a theme other than to show the Pechanga culture with the subtle influence of permanency and good taste. The spacious, high-ceiling interior of the hotel and casino is accentuated with a large oak tree in the main lobby created by naturalist/sculptor Bennett Abrams. There is abundant use of natural wood panels with hardwood trim, accented with aged copper accessories and brilliant red carpeting covered with oak leaf patterns. Also strategically placed through the complex are large picturesque murals created by artist Paul Price.

Pechanga claims to have the finest air cleaning and conditioning system available. This complex air handler, which cost $7 million, completely replaces the air every three minutes. Chances are patrons will not note any difference from the smoking to nonsmoking areas.

Goods and services purchased by Pechanga last year amounted to over $33 million, and $29 million was paid out in payroll for its 1,500 employees (fewer than 5% of whom are Indian.) With the opening of the new casino and hotel, employment exceeds 2,500 with a resultant 30-40% increase in payroll and purchases. These monies mostly go back into the local communities. Pechanga, now the second largest employer in the Temecula area, is well recognized for its contributions to local communities. They received the highest honor for their accomplishments in 2001 — the Platinum Large Business Award by the Temecula Chamber of Commerce.

The Pechanga Band has also greatly enhanced its services and support of its own community. They opened a new government center building in November 2001, about one mile from the hotel/casino complex.

GAMES

The gaming floor occupies about 85,000 square feet. Attractive areas of slots and videos include 2,000 of the most popular and the latest games like Monopoly®, Yahtzee®, and Wheel of Fortune®. Players can find slot machines for whatever level of bet is preferred, from 5¢ up to $25 denominations. The casino pays out over 10,000 jackpots every week.

Placed in pockets throughout the casino are 63 table games, including no-collection blackjack, with limits of $5 to $5,000. Pechanga Stud is one of the favorite table games; it's played like 5-card stud poker, but with three cards. The full service poker room, a favorite of serious poker players, has daily poker tournaments. The poker room has its own space for 17 poker tables and offers tournament play.

Courtesy Pechanga Resort and Casino

Blackjack tables at Pechanga

The High Limit Gaming Room has 22 favorite slots from $5 to $100, and three blackjack tables with a $100 to $5,000 betting limit. They cater to the "high rollers" who appreciate receiving personal attention while gambling for larger purses in privacy.

Bingo has its own spacious, well-equipped, and comfortable room that seats 700 players six days a week (closed Monday). Monitors are available for those who wish to supplement the card play on a video screen. Large action displays makes following the progress of play very easy from any seat. There is a Bingo Club for players to receive special offers, points toward merchandise, and other club benefits.

High Stakes Bingo and Jackpot Bingo add excitement for serious players. On weekdays sales start at 4 p.m. and games begin at 6 p.m. Early Bird cards are $5 for six cards while regular session cards are $20 for 12-on, with special prices for Power Bingo and Power Touch. On Sunday sales begin at 10 a.m., and Early Birds have a 12:30 p.m. start. All buy-ins receive a Pechanga "P" card free.

The Pechanga Player Rewards Club offers customers points for prize merchandise at wholesale prices. Players earn Rewards Club Points for every $1 in slot play and every $2 in video poker play. They are credited with $5 for every 5,000 points accumulated. Points are easily converted into cash or wholesale-priced prize merchandise. Qualified club members receive special monthly mailings, free or discounted rooms, tickets to entertainment venues at the Pechanga Resort and Casino, VIP line passes, exclusive invitations to promotions and special events, no wait express check in, and free food and beverages.

Courtesy Pechanga Resort and Casino

Hotel at Pechanga Resort and Casino

Two gift shops sell souvenirs, necessities, publications, hats and T-shirts, and other items. One is located near the hotel lobby and the other is adjacent to the theater/showroom.

HOTEL

The newly opened 14-story hotel has 522 luxury rooms and suites, a swimming pool, spa, fitness center, and other amenities, which make it a serious competitor with major California hotels. As far as local competition is concerned, for 25 miles or more, there is no comparable alternative. Besides being a comfortable abode for its gaming customers, the hotel provides first-rate facilities for conventions and entertainment seekers. Complexes such as Pechanga are no longer limited to day-trippers. They will attract a new group of visitors to the Temecula area from far and wide. The demographics suggest a draw mostly from California, but its reach will extend up the West Coast. The convention center has a total of 40,000 square feet including 13 meeting rooms, a tiered 125-seat lecture and teleconferencing room, and a 24,000 square foot hall, which doubles as a ballroom and can be subdivided into smaller sections. There is also a 3,000 square foot rooftop ballroom that can be used for meetings or special events.

RESTAURANTS

From the lobby area begins a parade of six luxurious restaurants to suit all tastes and needs. The 155-seat Great Oaks Steakhouse is one of few in the area to serve certified Black Angus beef along with other choice fish and poultry selections. The room, with its large central fireplace, provides quiet and comfortable elegance with fine wines and superb food. Reservations can be made here and are suggested, especially on the weekends. Call (888) 732-4264.

Paisano's Italiano specializes in both northern and southern Italian cuisine. This more festive environment with seating for 134 serves a wide selection of entrées to satisfy the palate of the most discriminating diners. The menu offers everything from pasta to veal and seafood to poultry.

The Seafood Grotto puts you in the mood for its specialties as soon as you step through the fishnet exterior into its comfortable surroundings. The chef creates taste treats from a variety of fresh Pacific fish, lobster, crabs, oysters and clams. Meals include delicious soups, salads, pastas, and potato choices. The Seafood Grotto shares a huge wall of man-made rock with the casino. In the restaurant the rock has the appearance of well-eroded red bluffs of the desert, while on the casino side it appears as massive rugged gray rock, such as seen on local mountains.

For flavorful food and a highly charged atmosphere visit the Blazing Noodles, which seats 120. It is Pechanga's answer for its valued Asian customers and for all who enjoy Oriental dishes.

The Buffet seats 450 and offers great food, great variety, and great prices. Diners will find a feast of foods from around the world. On Monday through Thursday the lunch is $8.49 and dinner is $11.49. On Friday lunch is $8.49 and the seafood dinner is $16.49. On Saturday there is breakfast for $7.99, lunch for $8.49, and dinner for $16.49. Sunday brunch and dinner buffets are $11.49.

The Pechanga Café, the first restaurant just off the hotel lobby, is open 24 hours a day and accommodates 192 diners. Everything from scrambled eggs to filet mignon can be enjoyed in a relaxed, friendly atmosphere.

Completing the food service options is the Snack Bar, for quick, light food and beverage items. It is located near the center of the casino floor, adjacent to the Pechanga Showroom.

If you visit on the weekends, be prepared to wait regardless of which restaurant you choose other than the Great Oaks Steakhouse, which is the only one that takes reservations. The Temecula area is short of good restaurants, and since the casino's opening their restaurants have attracted large numbers of hungry diners.

ENTERTAINMENT

Theater and show goers are in for a great treat when they attend performances in the 1,200-seat, multitiered, amphitheater style Pechanga Showroom, which offers excellent, up close, unobstructed views and flawless acoustics. The 14,000 square foot showroom features top name entertainers and Broadway musicals on a regular basis. Other live entertainment will be presented in the Cabaret Lounge, a more casual lounge show environment. The Cabaret,

Cascade, and Acorn lounges are adjacent to the casino floor and the fourth, called the Eagle's Nest, is on the top floor of the hotel.

RECREATIONAL VEHICLE RESORT

This facility opened March 2000 to provide RV travelers with the best services and conveniences possible. There are 170 full-service sites (24 pull-through sites) surrounded by lushly landscaped grounds. Sites are up to 45 feet long with room for a tow car. Services include: power, cable TV, sewer, and water hookups along with complimentary Internet access lines.

The recreation area has a common room with refrigerator, oven, microwave, and sink. The adjoining patio features a full-sized BBQ, year-round heated pool, and two spas. It also has a laundry facility with washers and dryers and convenience vending in the lobby. The RV resort area is conveniently located near the Pechanga gas station.

BUS SERVICE

Pechanga does not run its own buses or otherwise provide bus service from local communities, but it does work with tour operators to accommodate special group travel.

PECHANGA GAS STATION AND MINI-MART

The gas station and mini-mart, which opened January 1998, is located on the southeast corner of the property on Pechanga Parkway. They have 16 self-service pumps: 10 gasoline only, 4 diesel, and 2 gasoline and diesel. The mini-mart has an excellent selection of popular food items and accessory products for the traveler. A drive through automated car wash with coin operated vacuum service completes this facility.

Before leaving the Pechanga casino you may wish to take advantage of one of the hotel's 500 plus luxurious suites and rooms and enjoy an overnight stay before moving on to the next destination, the Cahuilla Creek Casino at Anza.

As you leave Pechanga, turn left on Pechanga Parkway and then turn right where it ends. You will be headed east on SR 79. The settlement of Aguanga is about 12 miles ahead. Look sharply because you won't find much more than a couple of small stores. Aguanga is famous for the historic battle between the Luiseño and Cahuilla Indians known as the Aguanga Massacre, a bad day for the Luiseño. A short distance from Aguanga, turn left (north) onto SR 371 toward Anza. Before you reach Anza, you will enter the Cahuilla Reservation and will spot the large sign for the Cahuilla Creek Casino on the right side of the highway. At an elevation of 4000 feet the high desert air is clean and crisp, and on cloudless nights the heavens seem much closer.

CAHUILLA CREEK CASINO

Cahuilla Creek Casino, 52702 Highway 371, Anza, CA 92539
Owned and operated by: Cahuilla Band of Mission Indians
Directions: From I-15 in Temecula take SR 79 east to SR 371 north
Telephone: (909) 763-1200
Website: www.cahuilla.com

Parking: **Valet:** No   **Indoor:** No   **Outdoor:** Yes
Bus service: No
Age for admittance: 21
Player's club: No
Nonsmoking area: No
Complimentary nonalcoholic drinks: No
Alcoholic beverages: Yes
Gift shop: Yes, gift counter at restaurant
Entertainment: Yes, lounge, dance floor, outdoor arena
Restaurants: Yes, 1, café
Casino size/gaming floor: 11,000/6,000 square feet

Table games: 3
Slots & video games: 207
Bingo: No
Offtrack betting: No
Poker room: No

Hotel: No
Golf course: No
Special attractions: Call or check the website for special events; day
    care center for children

SUMMARY 13

CAHUILLA CREEK CASINO

The Cahuilla Creek Casino is owned and operated by the Cahuilla Band of Mission Indians in the high desert on SR 371 in Anza. It's a small, unpretentious, country style casino with a down-home atmosphere. Though small, it does not lack in character. It is one of the most friendly and intimate casinos on the Jackpot Trail. You have a sense that this is the place where local residents as well as travelers enjoy getting together and hanging out. Their slogan, "The Friendliest Little Casino in the West," is not just advertising hype.

TRIBAL HISTORY

For general history of the Cahuilla, see Chapter 1 in this book. The Cahuilla Reservation was established by an executive order in 1875. It lies on the site of the ancient village of Paui, within the aboriginal territory of the Mountain Cahuilla.

Since 1877 there have been some changes in the ownership of the 19,000-acre reservation. According to a government report, only 2,000 acres are now held in common by the tribe. Individual members of the tribe hold the balance. Individual ownership of a large portion of this land makes for some interesting propositions as those with land titles seek ways to exploit their holdings. Apparently the casino venture, a tribal enterprise, is the only significant economic

Courtesy Cahuilla Creek Casino

development thus far. Providing leadership for the growth of the enterprise is tribal chairwoman Eugenia Nogales.

CASINO AND GAMES

This intimate gaming spot has 207 slots and a few tables to satisfy basic gambling interests within its 15,000 square foot tent-type structure. They have the usual popular Las Vegas style slots, including a set of Wheel of Fortune® 5¢ machines, video poker, reel types, and other progressives including Pot O' Gold® multigame machines. Most games are of 5¢ and 25¢ denominations with fewer numbers of $1 machines.

The casino has slot tournaments every Wednesday night beginning at 7 p.m. With their participation in progressive jackpot pools, they can legitimately claim to offer the highest rewards. Although not offering the greatest diversity, there's something to be said about not having to wait in long lines to cash out.

Just to the right-hand side of the entry is an enclosed area for the three table games. Blackjack is the game of choice, but you might get the friendly dealers to whip up a game of Pai Gow or something else that strikes your fancy.

It wouldn't be quite accurate to say they have a gift shop, but they do have a good selection of gifts in showcases at the restaurant. These include fine Indian style jewelry and other Indian items, T-shirts, caps, and more.

Photo by David Valley

Signage for Cahuilla Creek from the road

RESTAURANT

The dining room occupies a significant portion of the left side of the casino and, while not enclosed, its arrangement of café style tables with linens creates an intimate environment. They serve a wide range of menu items and beverages at reasonable prices for breakfast, lunch and dinner. Monday through Saturday they serve a breakfast buffet for $1.99. Thursday nights, beginning at 5 p.m., they offer a $8.95 buffet with country fried chicken, ham, roast beef, BBQ ribs, salads, potatoes, veggies, and desserts. For spicier flavors diners can choose from Mexican specialties of tamales, enchiladas, chile rellenos, tacos, and frijoles, or Italian dishes of antipasto, stuffed shells, lasagna, manicotti, sausage, meatballs, and pastas. The buffet does change some from week to week, so you may wish to call ahead to get the latest menu. They always serve great desserts including pies, cheesecake, carrot cake and ice cream specialties.

Sunday brunch features a grand assortment of early day specialties of omelets, Mexican machaca, bacon, sausage, fried chicken, potatoes, waffles, fruit, juices and other delights. Brunch is served from 8 a.m. to 2 p.m. and costs $5.95.

ENTERTAINMENT

Cahuilla Creek Casino brings excitement to the high desert with premier events, such as national professional bull riding competitions and championship ring matches of the Cobra Fighting Federation. The federation is known for its full contact bare-knuckle brawls and famous "Ring Girls." Music shows and concerts are also presented. Since the events are not on a regularly scheduled basis and vary in content, call (909) 763-1200 to see what is coming up next.

On a more regular basis customers enjoy Club 371, adjacent to the restaurant. This open style, multifeatured club has a bar with a neighborhood atmosphere, a place to shoot pool, a stage for live entertainment, and a good-sized wooden dance floor. There is TV to watch, and all drinks are reasonably priced. Sunday night is for karaoke singers. Dancers enjoy "oldies" on Tuesday night and live entertainment is offered on most Thursday, Friday and Saturday nights.

OTHER FEATURES

Cahuilla Creek offers a unique service among casinos, a day care center for children to use while mom and dad enjoy themselves. It is well equipped with toys for kids and a climbing playground for the little tots.

CHAPTER 8
VALLEY BRANCH
SAN DIEGO COUNTY

The Valley Branch, which includes five interesting and diverse casinos, provides one of the most scenic excursions on the Jackpot Trail with its heavily wooded areas and impressive mountains. Traveling south from Temecula on Interstate 15, after the mountain pass, you'll begin a descent into the San Luis Rey River Valley. Just before the river, take SR 76 east to the first stop on the Valley Branch. The road follows the meandering course of the river about five miles before reaching the Pala Reservation.

Map 9. Valley Branch

PALA CASINO

Pala Casino, 11154 Highway 76, Pala, CA 92059
Owned by: Pala Band of Luiseño Indians
Operated by: Jerry Turk
Directions: Interstate Highway 15, north from Escondido, Pala exit,
    SR 76 east, about five miles
Telephone: (877) 946-7252 toll free
Website: www.palacasino.com

Parking: **Valet:** Yes   **Indoor:** Yes   **Outdoor:** Yes
Bus service: Yes, tour buses only
Age for admittance: 21
Player's club: Yes, Pala Privilege Club
Nonsmoking area: Yes
Complimentary nonalcoholic drinks: Yes
Alcoholic beverages: Yes
Gift shop: Yes
Entertainment: Yes, 2 lounges, 2,000-seat events center
Restaurants: Yes, 6: steakhouse, café, buffet, deli, oriental, snacks
Casino size/gaming floor: 185,000/85,000 square feet

Table games: 50
Slots & video games: 2,000
Bingo: No
Offtrack betting: No
Poker room: No

Hotel: Scheduled for summer 2003 (507 guest rooms and suites; spa)
Golf course: No
Special attractions: Auto Service Station, Old Pala Village, Mission
    San Antonio de Pala, Pala Cultural Center (museum)

SUMMARY 14

PALA CASINO

P ala Casino, which is owned by the Pala Band of Luiseño Indians, was built from the ground up into a full-fledged Las Vegas style casino. The casino is conveniently located just five miles east of I-15 at the Pala exit, about 10 miles north of Escondido.

TRIBAL HISTORY

For the general history of the Luiseño, see Chapter 1 in this book. The 11,950-acre Pala Reservation was established by an executive order in 1875, becoming home for one of the San Diego County Luiseño bands. Today, the Pala Reservation is home to a mixed cultural group. In 1903 the Cupeño were displaced from their ancestral home because the hot springs located in their territory proved too attractive to white settlers. They were forcibly marched to the Pala Reservation, which was already inadequate to sustain the Luiseño band, and dumped there. The springs and area the Cupeño formerly occupied are known today as Warner Springs.

Mission San Antonio de Pala, which is only about a half mile north of the casino, was established in 1816 as an outreach of the main mission at San Luis Rey, a few miles east of Oceanside. The Pala Mission is remarkable in that it has been in continuous operation since its origin to the present time. Though heavily weathered and partially destroyed at times, it has been restored and maintained in its original appearance and purpose over the years. The mission

Courtesy Pala Casino

school was administered by various orders of the Roman Catholic Church until taken over in recent times by the Bonsall Union School District, which operates it as a charter school. The chapel and other buildings, including a museum and gift shop, are still in use by tribal members and others. The bell tower, modeled after a church in Juarez, Mexico, is a classic mission style with gently sweeping curves and belfry alcoves. The grounds, which include an old cemetery, are a beautiful and peaceful place to contemplate the history of generations past.

The chapel is a long and narrow room. Its white walls are made of adobe bricks and adorned with simple borders of brightly colored designs. The chapel has an open peaked roof of natural beams. The pews of dark rough wood on each side of the central aisle are plentiful and ready for congregants of the three Sunday morning services. The small altar has the usual trappings, but its centerpiece high up in the roof supports is a remarkable wood carving of a crucifix of the Savior. As you walk the length of the aisle and feel the depth of the irregular wear on the paving stones, you can't help but wonder about the multitudes of those who walked before you.

Located outside the chapel behind the bell tower is the cemetery with its dying flowers in tin cans, a pile of old wood fencing, and its barren hard-packed dirt cover. It invites attention to its eclectic mix of grave markers, from imposing granite monuments to weathered wooden crosses, some only a single vertical piece of wood reaching out of the ground like an outstretched arm. Hundreds of Indians and their padres were buried here many years ago, some in more recent times. The ground is consecrated by these blessed bodies and has been well watered with tears of remorse, regret, atonement, and hope. This is a sacred place to be treated with great respect.

The continuous operation of Pala Mission, even after the formal end of the mission system under the Mexican government, is a testament to the loving and caring support of many nuns and priests of the Catholic Church assigned to that outpost. Unlike the other missions, the clergy stayed on to provide support to the local Indians during that stressful disruption period.

The Pala Band, with meager government aid, has scratched out a living for its entire existence on the Pala Reservation. Though not rich in material possessions, the band maintained its strength, united in spirit and purpose through the lean years. With the advent of gaming opportunities, they planned wisely and have, in a relatively short time, established a thriving enterprise that will serve them well in the future. The tribal council is headed by Chairman Robert Smith.

CASINO HISTORY

Unlike other Indian bands and tribal groups that started as small bootstrapping operations and worked their way up the economic ladder step-by-step, Pala managed to make their first casino a significant and lasting one. A loan of

$100 million was arranged by Anchor Gaming, a major Las Vegas gaming enterprise that packages gambling operations and manufactures slot machines. They established Anchor Pala Development LLC (APD), a wholly owned subsidiary that is the loan guarantor, based on an operating contract with the Pala Band. APD partnered with the well known and highly experienced Jerry Turk to manage the operation.

The casino opened in April 2001 and has been going strong since then. The facility has a staff of 1,300 serving customers in their 185,000 square foot casino property.

The architectural style is reminiscent of Frank Lloyd Wright's designs with its clean graceful lines and open interior space. Mammoth windows overlook spacious verandas, Pala Lake, and the nearby mountains. The stylish interior is accented with colorful splashes of carpeting and capped off by grand chandeliers.

Finish work is done in natural color tones and materials including wooden beams and raw wood tongue and groove ceilings. Majestic porte cocheres at the main entrance and for the parking entries on the east and west sides of the main building beckon arriving guests. There are 3,000 parking spaces on the property for patrons, one-half of which are enclosed in an adjacent multilevel parking structure.

Not content to rest on their laurels, Pala will continue to develop as a first-rate resort. In the summer of 2003 they will open a four-star hotel and spa. The luxury hotel will feature 507 elegant guest rooms and suites, two new restaurants, and a 10,000 square foot day spa, offering a full range of spa services.

GAMES

Pala offers 2,000 Las Vegas style slots and 50 table games. Pala has one of the largest selections of slots available, in a variety of denominations including 2¢, 5¢, 10¢, 25¢, 50¢, $1, $2, $5, $10, $25 and $100.

Their new ticket pay system is available on 88% of the machines making it easy for slot players to move from game to game without the hassle of coins. Players simply receive winnings on a ticket, which can be used on other machines or redeemed at the cashier or at any of the 14 redemption windows throughout the casino floor.

The casino continually upgrades their videos and slots to new games, with more exciting features for players. Hollywood Squares®, $1,000,000 Pyramid™, Marilyn Monroe™, Survivor®, and American Bandstand® are some of the latest video game additions to the floor.

Reel type slots include great favorites. The popularity of the three coin $1 Double Diamond® progressives continues to increase. This classic game was made even more exciting at Pala by the addition of the progressive feature. This machine is hit on an average of once a day at Pala.

Quarter 5 Times Pay machines offer a chance to win a progressive jackpot with a bet of three quarters. These machines are located near the Promenade Lounge in the heart of Pala Casino. Since their recent introduction, customers have been playing them heavily in anticipation of being the next progressive jackpot winner.

Pala offers 58 Blazing 7s® machines in $1, $2 and $5 denominations. This game has been red-hot since the Pala opening and continues to be one of the most played games in the casino.

The popular Wheel of Fortune® game theme is offered at Pala in both video and reels. Videos can be played in both 5¢ and 25¢ denominations. The reel version is offered in 25¢, $1 and $5 denominations.

Pala's 50 table games, clustered throughout the gaming floor, deliver the variety of games and action the customers are looking for in today's casinos.

Blackjack is played like the major strip casinos in Las Vegas for various minimum bets. Mini-baccarat, the classic high stakes games where players may choose to wager on the player, banker, or a tie, is growing in popularity. Pala also has a "no commission" game. Pai Gow poker is offered at many tables. Caribbean Stud® poker, is an exciting variation of 5-card stud poker.

Players receive bonus payouts for wagering on the progressive jackpot. For example, in the exciting poker game Let It Ride®, players may take back their first and second bets as cards are being revealed or they can "let it ride." Players pursue the best poker hand using three cards of their own plus two community cards. There is also a $1 bonus bet that pays up to $20,000.

The latest craze in table games is 3-card poker. Players are dealt three cards and are allowed to make three different bets. Players make their best poker hand from three cards. There is similarly a $1 bonus bet that pays up to $20,000. Casino War is a simple, fast moving game fashioned after the old favorite where players turn over cards, one at a time, and high card wins.

For the comfort and convenience of its customers, Pala provides a very large nonsmoking floor area. For the "high roller" there is a special high-limit gaming area.

Pala's player's club is called Privileges. Players earn credit dollars on their favorite slots, video and table games. Credit dollars can be spent in restaurants, at the Impulse Shoppe for merchandise such as specially designed logo items, and to purchase tickets for concerts and for special events. Privileges Club members also qualify to receive invitations to parties, tournaments, and other special events.

RESTAURANTS

Pala has a good variety of restaurants centrally located in a spacious airy section of the casino. They legitimately boast that the food and beverage service is on a par with California's best restaurants.

The Oak Room at Pala Casino has become a world-class steakhouse, offering dry-aged, prime select steaks and chops, as well as fresh fish, lobster, veal and chicken entrées. Diners enjoy rich, warm surroundings with an attentive staff to assist them. An extensive, reasonably priced wine list and delectable desserts complement the meal. Hours are Sunday through Thursday 5-10 p.m. and Friday and Saturday 5-11 p.m. For reservations, call (877) 946-7252.

At the Terrace Buffet an amazing 60 different hot and cold food items are prepared fresh on site in an exhibition kitchen. This hearty buffet is served by a staff of 12 chefs. It features a full American barbecue, wood-fired pizza, many other specialties, and homemade desserts from Pala's on site bakery. Indoor and outdoor diners enjoy views of beautiful Pala Lake and nearby mountains in a relaxed atmosphere. The lunch buffet, served Monday through Friday from 11 a.m. to 3 p.m., is $8.99 while the dinner buffet, served Saturday through Thursday from 4 p.m. to 10 p.m., is $12.99. The Friday seafood dinner buffet is $18.99. Brunch on Saturday and Sunday, served from 9 a.m. to 3 p.m., is $11.99.

Pala Café serves a California cuisine in a bistro setting that includes fantastic salads, gourmet pizzas and burgers made from freshly ground Black Angus beef. Also on the menu are steaks, specialty sandwiches, and much more. Seating is available indoors and outside on the Pala Terrace. The café is open 24 hours every day.

The Deli claims to offer California's finest sandwiches prepared and served with a New York flair. They are over-stuffed, loaded with lean and flavorful meats. All breads are baked fresh in Pala's on site bakery and served with choices of premium cheeses, fresh condiments, leafy salads and crisp dill pickles. Hours are Sunday through Thursday, 11 a.m. to 11 p.m., and Friday and Saturday, 11 a.m. to 2 a.m.

Courtesy Pala Casino

Outdoor dining patio at Pala Casino

Coffee 'n More serves up hot combinations of Starbucks coffees, teas and cocoa, plus freshly baked goods, ice cream and shakes. Hours are 7 a.m. to 11 p.m. weekdays and 7 a.m. to 1 a.m. on weekends.

Noodles presents traditional Asian dishes from China, Vietnam, Thailand and Japan. The quick-serve style of authentic soups, noodles, barbecue and rice dishes are sure to please the most discerning palates — especially those hankering for that "oriental" taste. Hours are Sunday through Thursday, 11 a.m. to 11 p.m., and Friday and Saturday, 11 a.m. to 2 a.m.

ENTERTAINMENT

Pala Casino has three venues to appeal to those seeking entertainment and relaxation. The Pala Events Center presents national headline entertainment acts and sporting events with comfortable seating for 2,000 guests. Its contemporary sound and lighting systems enhance every entertainment experience.

Palomar Lounge, named for the mountain that dominates its floor to ceiling views, has an art deco look reminiscent of New York's legendary Radio City Music Hall. The stage is round to serve an intimate audience of 240 inside the lounge and, optionally, an enlarged capacity of 360 outside by opening an intervening wall. Palomar Lounge is wired for big screen TV broadcasts and closed circuit transmissions.

The Promenade Lounge has a contemporary California design including comfortable sofas, overstuffed chairs and loveseats. The lounge features a raised stage for entertainment and a full-service bar. Patrons can listen to the soothing sounds of live jazz and other acoustic performances nightly in candlelit comfort.

BUS SERVICE

There are no scheduled buses serving the casino, but tour buses can be arranged through Transportation Services.

AUTO SERVICE STATION

The facility is located on the west side of the property.

The next stop on the Valley Branch is only six miles to the east on SR 76. Be on the lookout for the casino sign indicating a turn to the left (north), just opposite a red and yellow painted sign outside a taco shop. Casino Pauma is the sweetest spot on the Jackpot Trail. You will understand why, especially in the early summer, as you drive a half mile through an orange grove. When the blossoms are in full bloom, the fragrance is heavenly. And, the sweetness doesn't end there. When you reach the parking lot, scan the view to the south and west. From this elevated position above the valley, the panoramic view is a spectacle to remember. In the evening at dusk, a slight haziness settles in the valley and the pink glow of the setting sun is bright in the western sky. It will take your breath away.

CASINO PAUMA

Casino Pauma, 777 Pauma Reservation Road, Pauma, CA 92061
Owned and operated by: Pauma Band of Luiseño Indians
Directions: Interstate Highway 15 north from Escondido, Pala exit
   SR 76 east about 12 miles, turn left (north) on Pauma Reservation
   Road
Telephone: (877) 687-2862 toll free
Website: www.casinopauma.com

Parking: **Valet:** Yes   **Indoor:** No   **Outdoor:** Yes
Bus service: Yes, CalTrans (public)
Age for admittance: 18
Player's club: Yes, Palm Club
Nonsmoking area: Yes
Complimentary nonalcoholic drinks: Yes
Alcoholic beverages: Yes
Gift shop: Yes
Entertainment: Yes, lounge
Restaurants: Yes, 2: Café/Buffet and Snacks
Casino size/gaming floor: 65,000/35,000

Table games: 20
Slots & video games: 850
Bingo: No
Offtrack betting: No
Poker room: No

Hotel: No
Golf course: No
Special attractions: Call or check the website for special events; craps
   and roulette

SUMMARY 15

CASINO PAUMA

Casino Pauma is owned and operated by the Pauma Band of Luiseño Indians. This is one of the six bands of the Luiseño in southern California with casinos. Their modest casino is nestled in a citrus grove on the southern slopes of Palomar Mountain in the heart of Pauma Valley. Casino Pauma features 24-hour dining, live entertainment, and 24-hour gaming.

TRIBAL AND CASINO HISTORY

For the general history of the Luiseños, see Chapter 1 in this book. There are two familial clans at Pauma, the Majel and the Pachito. Pauma's last chief was "Uncle" Ray Pachito. As chief he served as one of the four elders and performed ceremonial duties. The chief was a loved and respected honorary leader who served for life, as compared to the chairman, who is more of an administrative leader that is elected by the band to serve for a fixed term.

The Pauma-Yuima Reservation, which is divided in four parcels in two segments on Mt. Palomar, has a total land area of about 6,000 acres. Yuima is high up on the mountain and has no residents. Pauma is fertile and its gentle slopes are well suited for agriculture. For many years the band, with the productive labor of tribal members, has developed and managed large citrus and avocado groves. The agricultural business, with its dependable annual income,

Courtesy Casino Pauma

serves as a good foundation for the band's 135 members, 40 of which reside on the reservation. All members of the Pauma Band live in Pauma Valley.

As the Pauma Indians saw other southern California tribes and bands moving into gaming, they extensively debated the merits of doing the same. Many members felt they should concentrate on agriculture while others spoke out for diversification and an opportunity to significantly increase income. A time-based window of opportunity eventually forced them to commit or forever give up the gaming option.

A spokesperson for the Pauma Band said they had to work around the clock to open the gambling operation on May 15, 2001. That day was the state's deadline to begin operating their slot machines or risk losing them.

Though still in its early stages, band members believe their tent-type casino has the potential to provide a decent standard of living for the band and support the educational aims of its younger members.

Chris Deavers, the tribe's chairman, and Richard Darder, Casino Pauma's chief executive officer, are the driving force behind the casino operations. They implement plans of the tribal council, which includes all members 21 years and older.

Their $40 million investment gives them a modest-sized casino of 65,000 square feet that employs about 450 people. Because of its close proximity to larger casinos at Rincon and Pala nearby, Casino Pauma must find its niche to attract enough patrons to make it a paying enterprise.

Competing with the big operators is not an easy job, but it is one Casino Pauma pursues vigorously by offering attractive specials and friendly personal service. When this author revisited the casino recently and went to the customer service desk for his player's card, which had been left behind a few weeks before, the attendant commented favorably on his wife's attire and even mentioned what she was wearing previously. That was impressive.

GAMES

The casino is lively and has a festive atmosphere, which is accentuated by its tropical island décor. Though having fewer than half the number of video slots of the large casinos, you don't feel anything missing, as the assortment of machines is very complete. In close proximity are about 850 reel and slot video games and 20 table games. Players will find the usual suspects and a couple innovative games first introduced to Indian gaming casinos at this location. These are the full-scale table games of craps and roulette. If you thought these were illegal in California, you are correct. Casino Pauma skirts the restriction by replacing the actual dice of craps with a pair of cards numbered 1 through 7. The roulette wheel is replaced by a stack of cards numbered 1 through 72 plus the O, OO, and a joker. Otherwise, the game plays just like the originals, and the tables and playing surfaces are replicas of what you would expect for these games.

There are more than 50 different varieties of video games and slots in denominations from 1¢ up to $5 games. Among these are many progressive games and more than 100 video poker games. For players that enjoy the table game of 3-card poker, you will probably enjoy Pauma's exclusive video version. For keno fans there are 80 or more video games.

The popular table games are blackjack, Pai Gow, and 3-card poker. Blackjack is played with double deck and six deck shoes. Limits are from $3 to $500 ($2 on Tuesdays and Thursdays). Players may double down on any two cards, re-split aces and "surrender" on shoe games.

The poker room offers players chances at 7-card stud, Texas Hold'Em, Crazy Pineapple, and Omaha hi-lo split. There are double jackpots every even hour, free food coupons given after three hours of play, and tournaments on Friday, Saturday and Sunday. The table games open at 4 p.m. and go on to early morning hours Friday through Sunday.

Casino Pauma offers the Palm Club for players to accumulate valuable points that can be exchanged for cash on your favorite slot or table. They send monthly newsletters with valuable coupons for special offers and bonus gifts.

RESTAURANTS

The Pauma Bay Café offers a variety of dishes, a relaxing tropical setting, exceptional quality and top notch service to pamper your senses. Seating is available indoors or out. The patio provides dramatic views of citrus groves

Courtesy Casino Pauma

Dining at Pauma Bay Café

and the Palomar foothills. The Pauma Bay Café offers a 95¢ breakfast every-day 6-11 a.m. and a great prime rib dinner for two, Sunday through Thursday, 5-9 p.m., for only $10.95. More dining specials include a senior (55+) lunch with 50% off the menu prices for Palm Club members and a night owl break-fast buffet Friday and Saturday from 11 p.m. to 2 a.m.

Casino Pauma claims the buffet, which offers all you can eat, is a price that can't be beat. The lunch buffet, served from 11 a.m. to 4 p.m. everyday, is $5.95, and after 1 p.m. senior player's club members receive a 50 percent dis-count. The dinner buffet, served from 5 p.m. to 10 p.m. Sunday through Thurs-day, is $7.95. Friday and Saturday the buffet features prime rib at $10.95. Alcoholic beverages are served to legal-age patrons.

Located outside the Pauma Bay Café is the Triple Seven Bar, which serves delicious sandwiches, hot dogs, salads, and a variety of drinks — in-cluding an espresso bar for a quick pick-me-up. Deli hours are Monday through Friday, 4 p.m. to 6 a.m., and Saturday and Sunday, 24 hours.

ENTERTAINMENT

The Red Parrot Lounge, located in the center of the casino, offers live entertainment Tuesday through Thursday from 7 p.m. to 11 p.m. and on Friday and Saturday from 8 p.m. to 1 a.m. Tuesday evenings are scheduled for karaoke singers and fans.

Your next stop on the Valley Branch will likely be a short one, as it is a stretch of the definition to call the gaming place a casino. The La Jolla Band themselves call the 600 square foot area in their Trading Post a "slot arcade."

The trip to the La Jolla Reservation Slot Arcade from Casino Pauma is about 20 miles to the east along SR 76. Note as you go the first five miles that you will see a highway intersection on your right, which is S-6, the road to Valley Center. You will be doubling back to this point after the stop at the La Jolla Reservation Slot Arcade.

Try your luck at the La Jolla slots, and then you might want to pick up a drink and a snack or maybe munch on a hot dog or hamburger before you move on to the next stop, the new plush Harrah's Rincon Casino and Re-sort. You will not find more contrast anywhere on the Jackpot Trail than between these two spots.

LA JOLLA RESERVATION SLOT ARCADE

La Jolla Reservation Slot Arcade, 22000 Highway 76, Pauma Valley,
   CA 92061
Owned and operated by: La Jolla Band of Luiseño Indians
Directions: Interstate 15 north from Escondido, go east on SR 76
   about 30 miles
Telephone: (760) 742-3066
Website: None

Parking: **Valet:** No   **Indoor:** No   **Outdoor:** Yes
Bus service: No
Age for admittance: 18
Player's club: No
Nonsmoking area: Yes
Complimentary nonalcoholic drinks: No
Alcoholic beverages: No
Gift shop: Yes, store merchandise
Entertainment: No
Restaurants: Yes, 1: grill and deli
Casino size/gaming floor: 4,000/500 square feet

Table games: No
Slots & video games: 30
Bingo: No
Offtrack betting: No
Poker room: No

Hotel: No
Golf course: No
Special attractions: General store, gas station, campground, RV
   park, outdoor recreation, water park, horse riding

SUMMARY 16

LA JOLLA RESERVATION SLOT ARCADE

The La Jolla Reservation Slot Arcade, owned and operated by the La Jolla Band of Luiseño Indians, certainly qualifies as the smallest Indian gaming enterprise in southern California, perhaps anywhere. It is located in their campground Trading Post just off SR 76. Unlike the other casinos it has limited hours of operation. It is open Sunday through Thursday from 8 a.m. to 8 p.m. and Friday and Saturday from 8 a.m. to 10 p.m.

The La Jolla Band of Luiseño Indians has been in the family recreation business for over 60 years since they first opened their campground to the public in the 1940s. Generations of Californians are familiar with this scenic and rugged mountainside location and the warm hospitality of the La Jolla Indians. When you enter the Trading Post ask for Mitzi Magante, the genial manager, all-around expert, and public spokesperson. Give her a warm "Hello Mitzi!" and let her know you are a first-time visitor making this stop on the Jackpot Trail.

TRIBAL HISTORY

For early tribal history, see Chapter 1. The La Jolla tribe and their progenitors have occupied the land on the southern slopes of Mt. Palomar for hundreds of years. Its location close to the headwaters of the San Luis Rey River, a pristine water resource, has provided benefits from ancient times to the present.

Reservation status began in the 1870s when parcels were designated in the Quechla Basin (the original name of the San Luis Rey River) for La Jolla, Rincon, Pauma, Pala, and San Pasqual Indians. Although the La Jolla Band recognizes their roots within the Luiseño tribe, they were only indirectly influenced by mission administration. Their remote location has served them well over the years as a haven and resource for survival. Less than half of the band's 650 members live on the 9,000-acre La Jolla Reservation. The tribal complex

Photo by David Valley

includes a small mission, cemetery, recreation fields, education center, and library. The tribal chair is Wendy Schlater.

Looking toward the future, the band signed a gambling agreement with the state in the year 2000 to keep its options open. After considerable study and debate the band decided to start small with about 30 slot machines in the Trading Post. Even so, it took a half-million dollar investment, no small change for this frugal band.

Unfortunately, the La Jolla Band's most prominent citizen and spokesman, Henry Rodriguez, died an untimely death on February 14, 2002. He drove his car onto the highway and was struck by an oncoming car. He could not be there for the opening of the new gaming venture in May 2002.

Henry was born March 5, 1919, on the La Jolla Indian Reservation. He often told how Palomar Mountain was his playground when he was a child. He also recounted how his people depended on the mountain, where each band had acorn grounds for their food supply. Henry joined the U.S. Army Air Force before the start of WW II and served until 1945. He later became involved in politics to fight for Indian causes and became a national authority on Indian water rights. He was one of the founders of the San Luis Rey Water Authority. Henry was an active environmentalist and pioneer promoter of healthcare for California reservations. Though he never had the opportunity to complete college, in 2001 his distinguished career won him an honorary doctorate from California State University San Marcos. For those interested in learning more about this remarkable man, there is a wonderful series of articles written by David Ross. They are in the *Valley Roadrunner* and on the Internet at www.valleycenter.com.[23]

"CASINO" AND GAMES

The slot arcade is just to the left of the entrance to the Trading Post in a room not much larger than a good size family room. The 500 square feet of enclosed space has closely packed rows of 30 machines and a cashier's cage. There are several popular name brand machines and some of the usual reel and video poker games. Denominations are from 5¢ up to $1.

The management is modestly proud and unpretentious about its small gaming operation. All tribal and staff personnel, from Mitzi Magante to the security people, are very friendly and well accustomed to dealing with transient customers. Mitzi, like many other tribal members, wears several hats. She is manager of the Trading Post and chairwoman of the band's gaming committee.

RESTAURANT, STORE, AND CAMPGROUND

This is not dining at the Ritz, but for hot and cold food specialties including hot breakfasts, hamburgers and hot dogs, deli sandwiches, and more, the Trading Post is a great place to satisfy your hunger. The eatery is just beyond the stacks of canned goods and other items travelers and campers look for in this rural location. Like a trading post of the old West, you can find just about anything there, and outside you can gas up your wagon.

The campground covers a three-mile section of the reservation that encompasses the San Luis Rey River and Cedar Creek just south of SR 76. The entrance to the campground is near the Trading Post.

The campground has facilities for RV hookups at $20 per night or for campers at $17 per vehicle for up to four persons. The daily use fee for vehicles is $11. Each vehicle must be registered upon entry and have an adult supervisor at least 18 years of age. Campers may select from over 700 undesignated sites that may be used on an "as available" basis. Fishing (without a license) and swimming are allowed in the river, and for real excitement there is a water slide.

Oak Creek Stables rents horses for $20 for a one-hour excursion on guided trails. Supplies are available at the Trading Post. For more information call (760) 742-1297.

After visiting La Jolla Reservation Slot Arcade, double back about 12 miles along SR 76 and take Highway S-6 south. In about a mile or so, you will find the large Harrah's Rincon Casino and Resort, just off the west side of the highway. The Rincon San Luiseño Band of Mission Indians has been in the gaming business for more than a decade. It has been a bumpy ride for them as their original entry was aborted. Later they teamed up with the experienced casino management of Harrah's, which has helped to lead them to their current success.

They have been operating in tent-type structures since opening three years ago, but those structures have been razed to make room for the new resort. Their grand opening was in August 2002.

Photo by David Valley

Entrance sign from SR 76

HARRAH'S RINCON CASINO AND RESORT

Harrah's Rincon Casino and Resort, 777 Harrah's Rincon Way,
  Valley Center, CA 92082
Owned by: Rincon San Luiseño Band of Mission Indians
Operated by: Harrah's Operating Company, Inc.
Directions: North from San Diego on I-15, exit in Escondido at Valley
  Parkway East, which turns into Valley Center Road, proceed
  approximately 8 miles, casino is on the left
Telephone: (877) 777-2457 toll free
Website: www.harrahs.com

Parking: Valet: Yes   **Indoor:** Yes   **Outdoor:** Yes
Bus service: Yes
Age for admittance: 21
Player's club: Yes, Rincon Total Rewards
Nonsmoking area: Yes
Complimentary soft drinks: Yes
Alcoholic beverages: Yes
Gift shop: Yes**Entertainment:** Yes
Restaurants: Yes, 6: steakhouse/seafood, oyster bar, oriental, café,
  buffet, coffee bar
Casino size/gaming floor: 60,000/45,000 square feet

Table games: 32
Slots & video games: 1,500
Bingo: No
Offtrack betting: No
Poker room: No

Hotel: Yes, 200 rooms & suites, swimming pool, exercise facility
Golf course: No
Special attractions: Call or check the website for special events; large
  gift shop

SUMMARY 17

HARRAH'S RINCON CASINO AND RESORT

T he new Harrah's Rincon Casino and Resort is a well styled modern resort complex that will give the Rincon Indian community an assured business enterprise for economic self-reliance. Harrah's Operating Company brings California its first nationally known casino management with top notch amenities and a long history of excellent customer service. The new $125 million casino and hotel resort is the only one of its kind between Barona in the south and Pechanga in the north and the first resort complex to open in San Diego County.

TRIBAL AND CASINO HISTORY

For an early history of the Luiseños, see Chapter 1 in this book. The Rincon Reservation, established on December 27, 1875, is home to the Rincon San Luiseño Band of Mission Indians who now number about 125 families. The reservation spans approximately 4,200 acres in Valley Center. The Rincon community strives to promote and protect the welfare of its members and provides services such as supplemental educational programs and the Indian Health Council clinic.

As the voice of the Rincon San Luiseño Band of Mission Indians, Tribal Chairman John D. Currier has imparted a vision of economic success for the band. His greatest ambition is to create an empowered community abundant with employment and educational opportunities. Currier spent his last three

Courtesy Harrah's Rincon Casino and Resort

terms driving the business and political goals of the band with hopes of accomplishing the dream of ensuring tribal members independent lives. As chairman, Currier presides over the Rincon general council and tribal council meetings. Currier is one of two directors of the Rincon Enterprise Board, which serves as liaison between the council and casino management.

The Rincon San Luiseño Band of Mission Indians established the Rincon Gaming Commission on July 25, 2000, as the responsible body for gaming activity and personnel regulation and selected Harrah's to serve as its management corporation. As the primary regulator of gaming on the Rincon Reservation, the band places its highest priority on protecting tribal assets, upholding the integrity of the games, and ensuring a safe and secure environment for guests and employees. Their goal is to support the community's educational, healthcare, housing, and elder care needs, and to bring basic services to its residents. Gaming provides the tribe with significant economic resources and ensures a strong future for the community.

Revenue generated by the casino will be used to build new fire and police stations as well as to enhance the existing Head Start educational program and the infrastructure of the reservation. The operation is projected to generate about 1,100 full time jobs with a total payroll of about $30 million a year.

The new bright, airy and colorful casino has 45,000 square feet devoted to gaming. Harrah's management claims it is one the best casino floors in southern California. No question, it is one of the most attractive from its 30-foot vaulted ceilings to the colorful array of machines, topped in places with vivid rotating neon signs.

Jay Snowden, vice president of casino operations, oversees daily operations to insure that things run smoothly, profitably and in accordance with Harrah's high standards. Jay is a relatively young man, but he has solid casino experience and a top notch academic background as a graduate from Harvard University. Jay has already served for two years at Rincon and previously was with Harrah's in Las Vegas, responsible for slot operations.

GAMES

The casino has over 1,500 of the latest and most popular slots and video games including name brands, video poker, and progressives with a wide range of denominations to suit all players. The stylish bars also have video games built right into the lustrous granite tops.

There are 32 table games including three for baccarat, which includes two smaller seven-seat tables and one larger nine-seat table. There are four Pai Gow tables, one of which is progressive bonus. Other specialty games are two tables for 3-card poker, and one for Let It Ride®.

They have 21 blackjack tables in operation. In the main casino they deal to six players at most tables and to five at the high stakes tables. Dealers use between four and eight decks except for the "Super Fun 21" which is a single deck game. Betting limits are from $5 to $2,000. From time to time Harrah's will host promotional and invitational blackjack tournaments.

The basic blackjack rules at Harrah's are: dealer hits soft 17, double down after split is allowed, double down any two cards, split aces twice, split non-aces up to three times.

Total Rewards, their player's club, is the only multibranded loyalty program in the gaming industry that recognizes and rewards customers across the country at all Harrah's properties. The program combines all of Harrah's player rewards and recognition programs. It is an enhanced awards customer loyalty program with transferability of player rewards. Harrah's believes that by developing one loyalty program across all four of its brand named properties, including Rio, Showboat, and Harvey's, it adds tremendous convenience and value to customers, which is especially appealing to those who play in different locations across the country.

RESTAURANTS

Diners have excellent choices to satisfy all tastes and pocketbooks at the six stylish, upscale restaurants, but they are not apt to find a "Las Vegas" subsidized restaurant here. For a fine multicourse dining experience, perhaps after a good winning streak, try the Fiore Steak and Seafood restaurant. They serve a fine aged beef and freshest Pacific seafood complemented by excellent

Courtesy Harrah's Rincon Casino and Resort

Front entrance to International Buffet

California wines. Hours are 6-10 p.m. Wednesday, Thursday, and Sunday, and 6-11 p.m. Friday and Saturday. The restaurant is closed on Monday and Tuesday.

Seafood lovers will enjoy the sprawling Oyster Bar, which serves oysters, mussels, prawns, lobster and crab fresh from the sea.

For good old American comfort food at its best, customers can enjoy the San Luis Rey Café. It is open 24 hours a day, seven days a week. They serve the basic American fare with a touch of international favorites like fajitas and pizzas, salads, and desserts.

The International Buffet, which is probably one of the most attractive buffet venue found on the Jackpot Trail, boasts an array of favorite dishes from around the world. There is a wide expanse and variety of American, Asian, Mexican, and Italian dishes including salads, appetizers, roasted, grilled, baked and braised meats, and delectable desserts. The buffet is $14.99 for dinner Sunday through Thursday, 5-10 p.m., and $19.99 for Friday and Saturday, 5-11 p.m. The lunch buffet, served Monday through Friday from 11 a.m. to 4 p.m., is $9.99. Saturday and Sunday brunch, served from 10 a.m. to 4 p.m., is $14.99.

For those who enjoy oriental foods, Harrah's introduces the Fortune's Noodle Bar. This is nothing like the neighborhood noodle shop — it is a sleek, upscale, Chinese restaurant. Many varieties of oriental foods are served including sizzling pan-fried noodles and soup-based noodle dishes with spicy barbecued meats. Hours are 11 a.m. to 10 p.m. Sunday through Thursday, and 11 a.m. to midnight on Friday and Saturday.

For a quick pick-me-up, the Club Cappuccino has richly brewed high quality whole bean coffees concocted into cappuccinos, mochas, lattes, and other beverages to serve with a variety of pastries, confections, and sandwiches. Its location close to the hotel lobby and elevators was selected with overnight guests in mind. Hours are 6 a.m. to 10 p.m. Sunday through Thursday, and 6 a.m. to 11 p.m. Friday and Saturday.

ENTERTAINMENT

The Oasis Lounge, which seats about 125, features nightly musical entertainment including big band, country, swing and salsa for your listening and dancing pleasure. It has a large stage, in proportion to the room, which gives patrons an intimate connection with the entertainers. It is open to the adjoining bar, which separates it from the casino floor, so patrons can see a bit and hear what is going on.

The Pavilion is an 800-seat special events and multipurpose center for entertainment, banquets, sporting events, concerts, business conferences, tournaments and VIP events.

The gift shop is one of the largest you will find in a casino and has an excellent assortment: colorful apparel items — mostly T-shirts with spiffy designs, gift items from small trinkets to large sculptures, an expansive display of books about travel and gaming, and many magazines, snacks, and more.

HOTEL

The modern resort hotel has 183 oversized rooms featuring one king or two queen beds and large luxury baths with separate tubs and showers. The rooms are very attractive and well appointed, all featuring views of the surrounding area with its massive mountains. The 14 premiere suites afford added spaciousness, luxury, and spectacular views of the beautiful countryside.

For recreation and lounging in the abundant sunshine, guests can enjoy a 35,000 square foot pool area, a 157,000-gallon swimming pool, and a poolside bar. Those kinds of numbers mean little to most, so let's say the pool is huge and has an interesting and practical flower petal design with many extended fingers to create a sense of separateness and privacy. For a more vigorous workout guests may use the well-equipped exercise facility.

Rooms were fully booked for the first few months after opening but now can be reserved at $150 to $200 per night — unless you happen to be a high roller eligible for a freebee.

BUS SERVICE

Local service is provided from the surrounding communities, and group tour buses are available by special arrangement.

After Harrah's Rincon Casino and Resort, you are on the way to the last stop on the Valley Branch, the Valley View Casino. Continue south along Highway S-6, which is known locally as Valley Center Road. Just after the highway jogs to the west, look for North Lake Wohlford Road and turn left (south). Within a half mile, turn right onto Nyemii Pass Road. The casino is to the right as you go up the steep grade.

Valley View Casino bears witness to its name from its lofty position overlooking wide expanses of lowlands to the north. If you enjoy large-scale landscapes, get out your camera, paint set, or sketchpad to record this magnificent view.

Valley View is considered a small casino, but it is not lacking in games or amenities. Their comfortable restaurants, Market Square Buffet and Café de View snack bar, offer a good range of food service. This is a great spot to finish your day in a relaxed atmosphere with a delicious meal and a glass of beer, wine, or your favorite beverage.

VALLEY VIEW CASINO

Valley View Casino, 16300 Nyemii Pass Road, Valley Center, CA
  92082
Owned and operated by: San Pasqual Band of Mission Indians
Directions: I-15 north from San Diego, go east on E. Valley Parkway
  in Escondido to Valley Center Road, turn right onto N. Lake
  Wohlford Road and right onto Nyemii Pass Road
Telephone: (866) 726-7277 toll free
Website: www.valleyviewcasino.com

Parking: **Valet:** Yes   **Indoor:** No   **Outdoor:** Yes
Bus service: Yes, two local routes
Age for admittance: 21
Player's club: Yes, VIP Club
Nonsmoking area: No
Complimentary nonalcoholic drinks: Yes
Alcoholic beverages: Yes
Gift shop: No
Entertainment: No
Restaurants: Yes, 2: buffet and snack bar
Casino size/gaming floor: 40,000/20,000 square feet

Table games: 10
Slots & video games: 780
Bingo: No
Offtrack betting: No
Poker room: No

Hotel: No
Golf course: No
Special attractions: Call or check the website for special events.

SUMMARY 18

VALLEY VIEW CASINO

The Valley View Casino, owned and operated by the San Pasqual Band of Mission Indians, sits on high ground in Valley Center with a spectacular view of the surrounding area.

TRIBAL AND CASINO HISTORY

For the general history of this Ipai group of the Kumeyaay, see Chapter 1 in this book. The original San Pasqual Reservation, approved in 1870 by President Ulysses S. Grant, encompassed 92,000 acres from Ramona to Mount Woodson and Highland Valley to Lake Wohlford. However, in 1901 many of the indigenous people were evicted when the U.S. Supreme Court failed to uphold Indian land rights treaties established with the Mexican government. In 1903 the government purchased land in San Diego County and relocated some of the Kumeyaay there. Later in 1910 several reservations were expanded, including San Pasqual's, but this action was clouded by surveying errors and government obfuscation, such that tribal people were unaware of their land ownership status.

In the early 1900s the band was dispersed and would probably have drifted into oblivion except for efforts of a few tribal leaders to maintain ties. As recently as 1954 the Termination Act tried to do away with some Indian lands, but descendants of those tribal members who kept their history alive, asserted their claim and succeeded in permanently establishing their reservation.

Courtesy Valley View Casino

Today, the reservation is comprised of five separate, noncontiguous tracts totaling about 1,400 acres in the rolling hills of Valley Center. The San Pasqual Band is proud of its heritage and history as well as the role its 350 members now play in the local community. About one-third of the band's members live on the reservation near the casino, and many currently work in the casino.

One of the tribe's most renowned members was Felicita, daughter of the tribal chieftain, Pontho. As a young girl in 1846, she witnessed the Battle of San Pasqual between General Stephen Watts Kearny's U.S. Army of the West and the Californio Lancers under command of Andrés Pico. The Mexicans dealt a serious defeat to the ill-prepared Americans who hastily gathered up their wounded and made a ragged retreat. Felicita saw that an American had been left behind, and she tended his wounds, keeping him alive. With the help of other tribal members she returned him to the American troops. A romantic depiction of this event was staged and played for many years in the early 20th Century in Escondido. Felicita was well known during her lifetime around Escondido, often coming to market with her husband in a burro-drawn cart. She lived to be over 100 years old and will always be remembered as her name graces many Escondido features.[24]

During the latter half of the 20th Century the San Pasqual Indians, like others in southern California, witnessed the era of major high-tech business expansion. This activity drove much of the state's economy but offered little or no prospects for the Indians. There were few options for economic development left at their disposal. One option was agriculture, but it could not even provide for their minimum sustenance. Without education, training, and financial resources, their reservation land held little promise for the future until gaming became a possibility. Beginning in 1993, they concentrated their efforts in this direction, and with the signing of the California Gaming Compact in 1999, they had concrete plans for their casino well underway. The tribal council, headed by spokesperson Allen Lawson, carefully monitors their growth.

The Valley View Casino, which is modest compared to some, opened in April 2001. They prudently started with about one third the number of slot machines allowed by the Tribal-State Compact and fewer than a dozen table games. In considering the larger competition in the area, they anticipated that their success would hinge on establishing good relations with customers and practical means for attracting them to Valley View. Major elements in their formula for creating a successful "neighborhood casino" are food service, transportation, and customer benefits via the VIP Club.

The 40,000 square foot permanent structure is well designed in a Southwest style and attractive, inside and out. Patrons entering the casino will note the high ceilings (which helps keep the air fresh) and the bright neon light treatments throughout the center section. Machine clusters are well distributed throughout the gaming floor. Many of the clusters are topped off with cascading neon lights, adding an exciting festive look. To the far end on the left side is the dining area with superb views of the surrounding valley. The casino also has a small area where live entertainment is occasionally featured.

GAMES

Their inventory of 780 slots and video machines provides just about all the variety and selections of popular games players are looking for today. They will find plenty of the name brands such as Regis' Cash Club™, The Addams Family™, $1,000,000 Pyramid™, American Bandstand®, Bewitched™, and many others along with an excellent selection of video poker machines, multi-game machines, and progressive jackpot games with prizes up to $1.5 million. There are plenty of 5¢ and 25¢ denomination machines, and a goodly quantity of $1 machines, mostly of reel type slots and video poker machines. For those who enjoy the jingle jangle of coins, they will find many 5¢ and 25¢ coin machines.

Along the central core of the casino are 10 table games featuring eight blackjack tables, including a single-deck game, one for Pai Gow, and the other for 3-card poker. Most of the blackjack tables are $5-$25, played with multiple decks from a shoe. One or two tables are provided for high stakes players at $10-$1,000. Many newcomers to blackjack and 3-card poker have found Valley View a good place to learn the games without feeling out of place. Dealers of this "neighborhood casino" are especially helpful to novices who can learn how to play without feeling intimidated.

They have had their share of big jackpot winners too. One lucky woman hit a $1.3 million slot jackpot on a progressive machine. Frequent special promotional prizes, such as automobiles, are given away to lucky club members or visitors completing a free entry form.

The VIP Club claims to give five times more cash back than other San Diego County casinos. One point is earned for every $4 played. Every 500 points earned is worth $10 cash back. Members can use their points to pay for meals at the Market Buffet, to qualify for bonus entries in the monthly give-aways, for invitations to members-only slot tournaments for qualifying members, and to participate in the VIP gift program. The club card also qualifies holders for a $2 discount on dinner specials. All club members receive a monthly newsletter.

RESTAURANT

The Market Square Buffet is Valley View's answer to the hungry man, offering a vast range of fine foods at remarkably low prices. They serve food specialties made famous around the world with dishes aplenty to satisfy everyone's taste. Separately themed food stations ensure that everyone can find their favorite dishes, whether they be Asian, Italian, Mexican or American. Diners may also enjoy a wide selection of taste delights to finish their meals at the expansive dessert station. A special sugar-free selection is also provided to accommodate those who are sugar sensitive.

The casino's approach to food service is based on the classic Las Vegas formula whereby customers are attracted to a casino by way of satisfying their appetites and desire to get a bargain. For the quality of the food and great variety of dishes offered, it is plain to see that food service at Valley View is subsidized by the casino.

The author's firsthand inspection of the $6.99 Sunday Lunch Buffet, which includes endless refills of nonalcoholic beverages (beer and wine may be purchased at a reasonable price), showed the extent of their offerings. The salad bar, which is found at two stations, had 18 specialty salads. There were 15 different entrees plus hand carved roast beef, roast turkey, and honey-baked ham. For dessert there was a choice of 20 different items plus a sundae bar. The quality of the food was as high as you can find anywhere, and the service was swift and friendly. Can you ask for anything more?

The restaurant is open seven days a week, beginning with breakfast service (menu only) 7 a.m. to 10:30 a.m., Monday through Friday. The chef's special breakfast is $1.99. Friday to Sunday they have the added feature of steak and eggs for $2.99. Lunch is served every day for $6.99 from 11 a.m. to 4 p.m. The dinner buffet is $9.99 and served from 5 p.m. to 10 p.m. on Sunday through Thursday, and 5 p.m. to 11 p.m. on Friday and Saturday. Children are welcome in the restaurant and may eat free if less than 5 years old. Those from 5 to 10 years of age may eat for $4.99.

To add interest to the buffet dinners, there are nightly specials: T-bone steak on Tuesday for $11.99, prime rib buffet on Wednesday for $11.99, steak and shrimp on Thursday for $11.99, and seafood favorites on Fridays for $13.99. All of the specials may be discounted by $2 for VIP Club members.

If you are not ready for a full meal, the snack bar Café de View, just outside the entry to the restaurant, has a limited selection of sandwiches, salads, pizzas, desserts, and beverages including aromatic designer coffees.

BUS SERVICE

The casino runs its own free buses Sunday through Thursday on two routes. The coastal route has stops in Carlsbad, Vista, San Marcos, and Escondido. The inland route stops in Poway, Mount Carmel, Rancho Bernardo, North Escondido, and East Escondido. Call toll free (866) 726-7277 for the schedule.

When leaving Valley Center, you may back track on S-6 and SR 76 to I-15, or you can continue on S-6 into Escondido for a more southerly intercept of I-15.

CHAPTER 9
SOUTH BRANCH
SAN DIEGO AND IMPERIAL COUNTIES

The last branch of the Jackpot Trail has three exceptional casinos in relatively close proximity near Interstate Highway 8. The fourth is a smaller
casino, 25 miles farther to the east on I-8. The fifth and last is about another 100
miles to the east at the Arizona border.

Starting at the most northerly point of the South Branch in Lakeside, you
will find the magnificent Barona Valley Ranch Resort and Casino. From I-8 in
El Cajon, take SR 67 north, about five miles. After crossing the San Diego
River bridge, the next road to the right (east) is Willow. Turn on Willow and
proceed about a mile to Wildcat Canyon Road, then turn left (north). For about
five miles you will traverse a steep winding road until you descend into the
wide plain of the Barona Valley.

Visitors to Barona can make a quick stop for whatever interests them or
they can book an extended stay to enjoy the fine hotel, golf course, casino and
other local attractions.

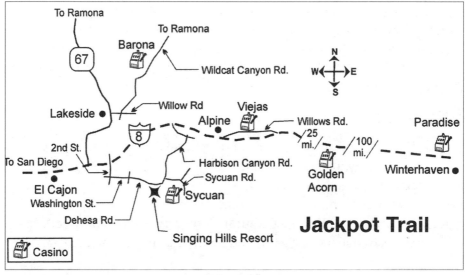

Map 10. South Branch

BARONA VALLEY RANCH RESORT AND CASINO

Barona Valley Ranch Resort and Casino, 1932 Wildcat Canyon
   Road, Lakeside, CA 92040
Owned and operated by: Barona Band of Mission Indians
Directions: Interstate Highway 8 east from San Diego, take SR 67
   north to Willow Road, turn right (east) for one mile to Wildcat
   Canyon Road, turn left (north), five miles to casino
Telephone: (888) 7-BARONA (722-7662) toll free or (619) 443-2300
Website: www.barona.com

Parking: **Valet:** Yes   **Indoor:** Yes   **Outdoor:** Yes
Bus service: Yes, tour buses, shuttle from El Cajon
Age for admittance: 18
Player's club: Yes, Club Barona
Nonsmoking area: Yes
Complimentary drinks: Yes
Alcoholic beverages: No, may be changed in future
Gift shop: Yes
Entertainment: Yes
Restaurants: Yes, 9: steakhouse, buffet, café, poolside snacks, coffee
   bar, burgers and malts, Mexican, pizza, and snack bar; food service
   also available on the casino floor
Casino size/gaming floor: 315,000/85,000 square feet

Table games: 52
Slots & video games: 2,000
Bingo: Yes
Offtrack betting: Yes
Poker room: Yes

Hotel: Yes, 364 guest rooms and 33 deluxe suites, swimming pool,
   fitness facility, business center, call (877) BV-RANCH (287-2624)
   for reservations
Golf course: Yes, championship course rated 4th in California
Special attractions: Barona Cultural Center and Museum, wedding
   chapel, gas station, car wash and auto detailing

SUMMARY 19

BARONA VALLEY RANCH RESORT AND CASINO

It is not difficult to ascribe the highest accolades to Barona above all other casinos in California, and most anywhere, based on its growing status as a world class casino and resort. Even before completion of the Barona Valley Ranch Resort and Casino, a $260 million project which opened in January 2003, Barona had all the pieces in place. The new facility has the most advanced gaming floor anywhere, a championship golf course, enclosed parking, 315,000 square foot casino, a luxury resort hotel with event and meeting facilities, and even a lakeside wedding chapel.

TRIBAL HISTORY

For the early history of the Kumeyaay, see Chapter 1 in this book. Capitan Grande was one of the early reservations established in San Diego County under an executive order signed by President Ulysses S. Grant in 1875. This 16,000-acre tract west of the Cuyamaca Mountains is named for the canyon through which the San Diego River once flowed east of San Diego. Indians from various bands of the Kumeyaay tribe resettled in this picturesque area with its large flowing river near present-day Lakeside. Indians from Mission San Diego were also given permission to locate on the reservation by the federal Indian agent, but few of them did so.

The new reservation land was not as expansive as the fertile valleys the Indians had left behind. It was largely unusable except for small areas along the San Diego River, which ran through it. Abundant water in these areas allowed the Indians to sustain themselves by farming, raising livestock, hunting, and

Courtesy Barona Valley Ranch Resort and Casino

fishing. Almost 60 years later the potential of this area as a reservoir to support the growing city of San Diego was recognized.

About 1930, the city of San Diego decided they needed the Indians' water resource, and they forced them to sell the land and move elsewhere. If this had happened 50 or so years earlier, chances are it would have been done without compensation, but by the 1930s there was some recognition of Indian property rights, and the city paid for use of the appropriated land. Once again land rights of the Indian inhabitants were dismissed, even though they lived on a federal reservation grant. The city of San Diego had claimed water use rights of the land by eminent domain. By exercising this "right," the city had actually taken the water even before they purchased the land.

When the city built Lake Cuyamaca, it constructed a flume through the Capitan Grande Reservation that took most of the San Diego River water originally used by the Kumeyaay. This left them only a small share from the city's flume that resulted in crop loses on Indian farms. The city later decided to dam the river and take all of the water by creating El Capitan Reservoir. The displaced Indians were given token compensation for their lands.

Within Capitan Grande Reservation were two distinct bands, the Capitan Grande group to the west and the Los Conejos to the east. These bands later became known by the names of the areas they purchased with resettlement money, which became their new reservations. The original Capitan Grande Reservation remains undeveloped and protected as an ecological preserve. Currently the uninhabited reservation is administered jointly by the two bands, the Barona Band of Mission Indians and the Viejas Band of the Kumeyaay Nation.

The displaced Capitan Grande band purchased a 5,200-acre ranch, about five miles to the west of the Capitan Grande Reservation and once again resettled. This land later became the reservation for the Barona Band of Mission Indians. The Los Conejos group purchased the Baron Long Ranch at Viejas.

The land purchased by the Barona Band did not have a large body of water, but its open plain had advantages for cultivation of crops, ranching, and hunting game. This provided the necessary subsistence for the band.

The origin of the Barona name, which was later applied to the band, traces back to Spanish settlers. According to *Legends of Lakeside*, the earliest Spanish landowners initiated the name. Records show ranch owner Juan Bautista Lopez was the first holder of the land grant. Later, in the mid-1800s, he deeded the ranch to José Domingo Yorba who gave it a Spanish name meaning, "glen of St. Vincent and mesa of Padre Barona" (of the San Diego Mission). Apparently the origin of the name was from this Spanish priest.[25]

A tribal member spoke of his youth there saying he didn't realize how poor they were. He remembered his childhood years on the "rez" playing in nature, as an enjoyable experience. No doubt his parents and grandparents would remember the harshness of living on the edge of survival until as recently as the mid-1980s.

In 1984 the Barona Band, after years of trying to find a way to improve their economic state, decided to enter into public gaming and offered bingo. During the next decade bingo paid the bills and established a credible financial foundation. In 1994 the major "Big Top" expansion heralded their entry into modern gaming, albeit with some testy times ahead as legislative issues were debated and resolved.

Today, Barona is one of the most successful Indian casinos in the country. The band is entirely self-sufficient, well cared for, and now on the giving end as the band is a very significant contributor to the local economy and charities.

NEW CASINO

The $260 million dollar resort, designed by Bergman, Walls & Associates, the acclaimed architects of Paris, Caesars, and the Mirage in Las Vegas, opened in January 2003. Nestled in the picturesque rolling hills of the Barona Indian Reservation, the resort's California ranch influenced design accentuates the rich cultural history of the Barona Band of Mission Indians and pays tribute to the founding fathers of the reservation that purchased the Barona Ranch in 1932. The theme is meant to create an impression of a sprawling and upscale 1930s ranch that has been evolving and expanding through the decades. Evocative natural imagery and elements reflect the tribe's harmonious coexistence with and reverence of nature. The dark wood and stone façades of the aged, ranch style building are designed to blend with the surrounding landscape and the existing structures on the Barona Indian Reservation. Most visibly memorable is the barn and silo structure of immense proportions that houses the all new 315,000 square foot casino. It is accented with a man-made lake in front of the casino featuring an eye-catching, pristine-white wedding chapel just off-shore. Other elements include a functioning old mill waterwheel, several lakes, and a period footbridge. According to Joel Bergman, president of the architectural firm: "This concept is not of a ramshackle farm, but rather a themed, carefully integrated facility such as the master himself, Walt Disney, would have created. Ranch life has never been this good."[26]

GAMES

The $1 million Barona StarDome™, the world's largest indoor casino signage ever built, lights the way to casino gaming excitement.

Video slots provide the full complement of 2,000 games allowed under the Tribal-State Compact and are of the latest and most popular varieties offered anywhere, fully equipped for coinless vouchers and club member credits. Whatever you favor, from the multifeatured name brand video games, such as Wheel of Fortune®, Monopoly®, I Dream of Jeanie™, to new games such as

Quartermania® and Raining Diamonds™ or the fast-paced, big jackpot spin-ning reel games such as Blazing 7s®, and Red, White, & Blue®, you will find them all — progressive, interactive, and traditional slot machines. *Strictly Slots Magazine* has called Barona Casino the "loosest slots in San Diego" for two consecutive years, and *Blackjack Forum Magazine* has rated Barona Casino "California's best high-stakes blackjack." Barona pays out an average of $10 million daily to lucky winners.[27]

Barona has game denominations to suit every pocketbook, from 1¢ to $500 slots. Penny Junction, created exclusively for Barona, can be played with bets of 1¢, 2¢ or 3¢. For players that still prefer the jangle of coins, there are also many coin-operated machines in the mix. Many of the games feature progres-sive jackpots that pay out millions of dollars, month after month, with running jackpots of $3 million or more. There are 200 multihand video poker games with machines for triple, 10, 50, and 100-play and also other poker variations and denominations. Video poker fans will find nothing lacking at Barona.

Table games, numbering 52 in total, provide variety and fast action. Black-jack is played with a choice of single deck, double deck, or six deck shoes. They also offer single deck high stakes blackjack with the surrender option. Pai Gow is coupled with American poker, played with a 52-card deck and a wild card joker. Casino War is one of the new simple games — just draw a card higher than the dealer's to win. Let it Ride® is a 5-card stud poker game that allows players to control two of their three bets and gives them an opportunity for big winnings with a $1 side bet. Three-card poker offers three ways to play

Courtesy Barona Valley Ranch Resort and Casino

Gaming at Barona Casino

and four different ways to win plus possible bonus payouts. Caribbean Stud®, is a 5-card stud game where the player tries to beat the dealer's hand. Table limits are as high as $5,000. The separate poker room, adjacent to the offtrack betting area, has 11 tables. Barona offers a variety of poker tournaments.

Bingo, the genesis of Barona gaming, is still going strong in a new 500-seat bingo parlor called Founder's Hall. The 20,000 square foot multipurpose room is partitioned into smoking and nonsmoking areas with a snack bar for the convenience of patrons. When not used for bingo, Founder's Hall is used for special events, concerts, and meeting space. Barona's bingo games are run in Las Vegas style one-hour sessions with a one hour break in between. Most play on paper, but there are electronic options available. Buy-ins are in the $10-$15 range for 10 cards with discounts early in the day. Bingo is played seven days a week, except on special occasions noted on the bingo calendar.

Offtrack betting is provided for horse racing fans in a well-equipped room with partitioned sections for smoking and nonsmoking. There are large 50-inch monitors for viewing major races and 27 smaller TVs covering the rest of the action.

Club Barona is a free club. All patrons should join to earn valuable points as they play any of the 2,000 slots. Points can be redeemed for cash, dining, hotel, merchandise, golf and more. Members receive special offers such as invitations to exclusive members only events and are entered into drawings to earn prizes. Sign up at the casino or on line at www.barona.com.

RESORT HOTEL

The new hotel, overlooking the scenic Barona Creek Golf Course, promises five-star service for guests enjoying the comfort of its 397 rooms, which includes 33 deluxe suites. For those who really want the full extent of luxury and spaciousness in a large home, there are four 4,000 square foot luxury suites. Each includes a private workout room, Jacuzzi tubs, two bedrooms, separate living space, private butler service, and dining room.

For groups of 25 to 600 persons, the hotel and events center staff can arrange everything including dining, reservations for a single night or plans for weddings, receptions, corporate conventions, and group meetings. Hotel amenities include an exercise facility, swimming pool, and full-service business center for the visiting executive.

GOLF COURSE

Though a newcomer to the California circuit, Barona Creek Golf Course has already been established as a top championship course, ranked fourth in California, just below Pebble Beach, Spyglass Hill, and Pasatiempo, and tenth in the country according to *Golfweek Magazine*.[28] Barona Creek was designed by Gary Roger Baird, Design International. It is an 18-hole, par 72 course of

Courtesy Barona Valley Ranch Resort and Casino

Hole No. 3, Barona Creek Golf Course

7,088 yards with about 100 multifingered bunkers and a series of lakes, ponds, and creeks. The golf course is nestled among 170 mature native oak trees that give character and challenge to the undulating terrain, replete with rock out-croppings and gentle elevation changes.

For pre-game practice, there are 10 acres of developed land, which includes a 12,000 square foot putting green, a 6,000 square foot chipping green, and a 40 space all grass driving range.

To satisfy Barona's concerns for environmental conservation, course de-signers included an integral $3.5 million wastewater treatment plant to provide reclaimed water for irrigation.

For tee times and reservations, call (619) 387-7018.

RESTAURANTS
The food service at Barona shows the culinary expertise of Executive Chef Scott Kidd and staff. The casino offers nine different dining options to satisfy the interests and palates of their customers.

The expanded Ranch House Buffet has over 200 menu selections daily with seating for 850, with 750 seats indoors and 100 on the patio, all of which offer a magnificent view of the Barona Creek Golf Course. The bright and festive décor sets the stage for an international cuisine with separate stations for Mexican, Asian, Mongolian, Italian, and American foods, with additional sta-tions for rotisserie, salads, and desserts. The types of food items at the interna-tional stations are changed daily, making each day's buffet a new experience.

The restaurant is open for brunch Monday through Thursday from 10 a.m. to 2 p.m. and on Saturday and Sunday from 10 a.m. to 4 p.m. The Friday buffet is open from 10 a.m. to 2 p.m. The cost is $9.99 Monday through Friday and $12.99 Saturday and Sunday. Dinner buffet is served 5-10 p.m. daily. The cost is $14.99 Sunday through Thursday and $16.99 Friday and Saturday.

Branding Irons Café, an upscale coffee shop, has a nice view of the golf course and the landscaped lakes of the Barona Creek Golf Club. It is open 24 hours a day, seven days a week. There are 230 interior seats in the café and another 80 on the patio — a great spot for lunch on any of the many pleasant days at Barona.

Barona Oaks is an 80-seat upscale steakhouse serving such intriguing menu items as buffalo ribeye steak, diamondback rattlesnake fritters, and red chili crepes. The décor is refined and tastefully done with shining hardwoods and granite-topped tables. It is open daily for dinner only from 5 p.m. to midnight.

Reflections is an appropriate name for the 125-seat poolside restaurant near the entrance to the resort hotel. Lunch and snacks are served in this outdoor setting when the weather is comfortable for swimming.

For patrons on the go who are looking for quick food service, Barona has a food court adjacent to the casino floor, with a 64-seat eating area. Sharing the honors are four quaint eateries. The Barona Coffee Company, specializing in coffee and homemade pastries, is open 24 hours, seven days a week. Fiesty Kates is a 1950s décor burger and malt shop, open daily from 10 a.m. to midnight. Sombreros serves Mexican food 24 hours a day. Da Boyz Pizza is the place for pizza, pasta and fresh salads. It is open from 10 a.m. until midnight.

Completing the food service to customers is the snack bar in the bingo room, which serves salads, sandwiches, burgers, hot dogs, and fries from 10 a.m. to 11 p.m. For hotel guests there is 24-hour room service. Items can be selected from a wide variety of choices in the room service menu.

Casino patrons who don't want to miss the fun and excitement of the casino floor can invite Lady Luck to dinner and enjoy "Jackpot Dining" — their meal can be delivered directly to their winning slot machine or table game.

BUS SERVICE

Tour buses can be arranged from any area in southern California. An individual's transportation charge can be waived, depending on their level of play. A shuttle bus is operated from El Cajon. Riders pay a $10 fee, which is returned to them in casino credits when they arrive. No municipal bus service comes to the casino.

AUTO SERVICE STATION

The service station on Wildcat Canyon Road is appreciated by those in need, as there is no other gas station for six miles or more in either direction. In addition to the service station on Wildcat Canyon Road, there is a car wash and detail service available at the casino. Attendants can give your car a wash or detailing while you play your favorite games. If you have accumulated enough points, you may use them to shine up the old wagon.

BARONA CULTURAL CENTER AND MUSEUM

Clifford LaChappa, tribal chairman, is rightfully proud of the recently completed Barona Cultural Center and Museum, which is located about one mile north of the casino property on Wildcat Canyon Road. He said, "During the last millennium, many Native Americans almost lost the knowledge of their history and culture. Because of Indian Gaming, we have the resources to restore our pride. With this museum, we can guarantee that our history will be kept alive."[29]

With its curated collection of artifacts from Barona tribal members and others, the Barona Museum is now home to over 2,000 ancient items that showcase the artistry and skill of Native Americans who lived throughout San Diego County and the West.

According to leading archaeologists, the collection housed in the Barona Museum represents thousands of years of Native American history. In fact, experts say some items date back as far as 10,000 years, with other pieces originating as recently as the 1930s. Going beyond the usual showcases, the museum provides listening alcoves, diorama displays, and interactive science presentations.

This is a great place for adults and school children alike to explore and learn most directly about Native Americans. The museum is open Tuesday through Sunday, noon to 5 p.m., or by appointment for tours and research. For more information, call (619) 443-7003, extension 219.

An historic site of import that can be seen when visiting the museum is the Barona Mission, a Catholic church across the street from the gas station. The mission and the original cottages built for the Indians during the 1932 relocation from Capitan Grande were designed by famed San Diego architect Irving Gill.

When leaving Barona, double back on Wildcat Canyon Road south to the I-8 freeway. Head east about 10 miles and look for the Harbison Canyon exit. Turn off there and proceed along the frontage road (east) to Arnold Way and turn right. This road will intercept Harbison Canyon Road, which descends steeply into the canyon below. Turn left (east) onto Dehesa Road, after a short distance take Casino Way to the right, down into an oak grove, then another left hand turn and voilà! The splendid Sycuan Casino and Resort is there before you. It rises up suddenly, like a mirage at a desert oasis, and looks like a sultan's palace. You may avail yourself of their valet parking as you drive under the massive portico or continue along the side of the casino to the large parking lot.

SYCUAN CASINO AND RESORT

Sycuan Casino and Resort, 5469 Casino Way, El Cajon, CA 92019
Owned and operated by: Sycuan Band of the Kumeyaay Nation
Directions: Interstate Highway 8 east, past El Cajon to the Harbison
   Canyon Exit, take Arnold Way to Harbison Canyon Road, 10
   miles, turn left on Dehesa Road (east) and right onto Casino Way
Telephone: (800) 279-2826 toll free for the casino and (619) 442-3425
   for Singing Hills Resort
Website: www.sycuan.com

Parking: **Valet:** Yes   **Indoor:** Yes   **Outdoor:** Yes
Bus service: Yes, Sycuan Express Buses from various San Diego area
   locations
Age for admittance: 18
Player's club: Yes, Club Sycuan
Nonsmoking area: Yes
Complimentary nonalcoholic drinks: Yes
Alcoholic beverages: No (in the casino)
Gift shop: Yes
Entertainment: Yes, Showcase Theater
Restaurants: Yes, 6: buffet, café, seafood, bingo snack bar, Turf Club,
   deli; dining also available at Singing Hills Resort
Casino size/gaming floor: 305,000/120,000 square feet

Table games: 60
Slots & video games: 2,000
Bingo: Yes
Offtrack betting: Yes
Poker room: Yes

Hotel: Singing Hills 102 rooms and suites, conference rooms, shuttle
   service, swimming, restaurants, alcohol service
Golf courses: Yes, 3: 2 18-hole championship courses, 1 par-3 course
Special attractions: Singing Hills Resort, 11 tennis courts

SUMMARY 20

SYCUAN CASINO AND RESORT

The Sycuan Casino and Resort is owned and operated by the Sycuan Band of the Kumeyaay Nation. Sycuan offers guests a complete package. The casino and its resort hotel, Singing Hills, cater to all their patrons' desires for gambling, fun, recreation and relaxation. The casino is about three miles distant from the resort hotel complex and is conveniently coupled by courtesy transportation services.

Sycuan is an attractively decorated full-sized casino, which has it all: 2,000 video games and slots, over 60 table games, a high limit room, offtrack betting, bingo, and entertainment. Alcoholic beverages are not served. Singing Hills has multiple golf courses, tennis courts, and a swimming pool to complement its luxury hotel. It has full bar service in its lounge and dining areas.

TRIBAL HISTORY

For the early history of the Kumeyaay, see Chapter 1 in this book. In 1875, President Ulysses S. Grant's executive order provided land in San Diego County for the Kumeyaay. The Sycuan Reservation, a 640-acre tract in Dehesa Valley, was included in this order and became the first Kumeyaay reservation in the county. This land, like much of the lands ceded to Indians, was remotely located and of marginal quality. It was difficult to farm and too small at one square mile for any sizable herd of grazing stock. Even so, some of the resilient Sycuan Band members managed to survive on the reservation land. Others, not on the reservation, managed to eke out a living on the fringes of white communities.

Courtesy Sycuan Casino and Resort

Were it not for the introduction of gaming, the Sycuan Indians would still be leading a life of poverty and dependency on a failed government welfare program. While not forgetting the past, the Sycuan people now look forward to the future and to enjoying the benefits of being self-reliant once again.

In addition to the casino, the small Sycuan Reservation has an old chapel, tribal cemetery, fire department, and a school. The seven-member tribal council enacts laws and promulgates regulations to ensure the health, welfare and safety of the tribe. The council also serves as the board of directors for business enterprises of the tribe. Council members serve four-year terms. Tribal members must be 18 years of age to vote. The current tribal chairman is Danny Tucker.

CASINO

The lavishly decorated 305,000 square foot casino, reminiscent of a Sultan's palace from its massive exterior features to its attractive and whimsical interior décor, sets the mood for comfort and fun as customers enjoy their favorite games of skill and chance and dine at delightful restaurants. The casino has had its share of big winners. Recently, an 85-year-old San Diego grandmother won a huge jackpot after playing only $31.50 in a Jeopardy!® quarters slot machine. Bernadine Ann hit the lucky combination and won $433,005.

In June 2002 the Sycuan Band selected Steve Penhall as the new general manager for the Sycuan Casino and Resort. He comes to Sycuan after serving three years as general manager for the Sandia Casino in Albuquerque, New Mexico. Prior to that, Penhall spent seven years at the Ute Mountain Tribal Casino near Durango, Colorado. Penhall entered gaming after a career in law enforcement.

GAMES

Video games and slots, arranged in convenient clusters, dominate the casino floor. There is a total of 2,000 Vegas style machines for all denominations of play. Sycuan has a great variety of favorites including Joker Poker™, Double Bonus Poker™, Austin Powers™, Monopoly®, Wheel of Fortune®, Jeopardy!®, The Price Is Right™, Elvis®, and The Addams Family™, just to name a few. Sycuan also features the largest nonsmoking slot room in San Diego.

For an unusual diversion, multiple players can "play the horses" as mini-models of their favorite steeds gallop around a track. For the more serious players, there are plenty of surefire spinning reel games and all types of video poker games.

There is no shortage of progressive jackpots at the Sycuan Casino, where first-time casino player Art hit the Quartermania® Jackpot for $1 million. Slot tournaments for video poker players are held Monday, Wednesday, and

Thursday. Players get a $1,000 credit for a $20 buy-in. The top 10 winners receive prizes from $50 to $1,000 and first place finishers are invited to a free champions tournament once a month.

Sycuan has about 60 table games and offers the popular games of black-jack, Pai Gow, Caribbean Stud®, 3-card poker, Let It Ride® and traditional open poker games. The Pai Gow room has cash bonuses every night, with jack-pots up to $7,500. For baccarat players there's the option for mini-baccarat with limits from $10 to $1,500, or big-baccarat in the high stakes room with limits from $50 to $5,000.

The poker room features 17 tables for poker and an elegant smoke-free setting to enjoy the competitive action of Omaha hi-lo, Texas Hold'Em and 7-card stud. Tournaments and special promotions are held weekly in the poker room, offering nonstop fun and excitement.

The new High Limit Room provides an attractive and comfortable envi-ronment for high stakes players. Open daily at 6 p.m., this exclusive facility offers double-deck blackjack with limits from $50 to $5,000.

The casino offers double jackpots for poker players every weekday at spe-cial times, and weekend tournament play on Friday, Saturday, and Sunday. A bonus Hi Stud Jackpot of $5,000 is paid out for any hand beating four eights or better and at the same time is added to the posted jackpot. For the early morn-ing poker players, there is a special $2 breakfast menu.

The Bingo Palace on the second floor of Sycuan casino can easily be said to be the most elegant bingo hall in San Diego. It seats 1,200 players in separate smoking and nonsmoking sections and offers daily jackpots during matinee and evening bingo sessions. In addition to playing on paper, guests can also play bingo on Sycuan's video bingo machines and use portable handheld units. Bingo at Sycuan is serious business with matinee and evening games sched-uled seven days a week. Matinees with $5 and $10 buy-ins begin at 9:30 a.m. Seniors get a $5 discount on the $10 buy-in for the matinee games. On Satur-day and Sunday all earlybirds (9:30 a.m.) get free breakfast. Evening games beginning at 7 p.m. offer $10 and $15 packs, plus the $3 bonus packs for pay-outs from $1,000 to $1,500. Twice a week there is a special $5,000 bonus jack-pot, and other promotions are held at various times.

Offtrack betting has been a long time favorite at Sycuan with its comfort-able lounge featuring large screen TVs. The facility is open during post times of popular racetracks across the country and for special events.

By using the Club Sycuan card throughout the casino, guests can earn points good for valuable rewards, including free meals, merchandise, and special dis-counts. Poker players can also win player's club points, but they must give their card to the attendant.

RESTAURANTS

Dining choices include a great buffet at Paipa's Oasis Buffet. It is an all you can eat treat of hand carved meats, Asian specialties, fresh salad bar, soups, and a decadent dessert bar for diners with hearty appetites. Different food specialties from around the world are featured everyday at Paipa's, named as San Diego's "Best Buffet" by the *San Diego Reader*. For dinner and Sunday brunch, prime rib of beef and peel-and-eat shrimp are offered as additional dining choices. Monday through Saturday the lunch buffet is served from 11 a.m. to 2:30 p.m. for $8.95. Dinner hours are 4-10 p.m. Sunday through Thursday and 4-11 p.m. Friday and Saturday. The all-day Sunday buffet is served from 10 a.m. to 2 p.m. Dinner and Sunday buffet is $12.95.

For a more relaxed full-service meal, diners may enjoy Wachena Falls Café. It offers the ambiance of patio dining with entrée choices to satisfy any taste. Choices are near limitless, including certified prime Angus beef, exciting pasta creations, your favorites from south of the border, and sandwiches and burgers. Start your meal with taste pleasing appetizers, and be sure to save room for delicious desserts. Whether you're looking for a full meal or a quick snack 24 hours a day, Wachena Falls Café is the answer.

Dine at the Turf Club while watching the action from racetracks all over the United States. Menu choices include, salads, sandwiches, burgers, and fresh pasta entrées — all brought to your table so you don't have to miss any of the exciting racing action. The Turf Club is open one hour before post time and closes 30 minutes after the last post time.

Pearls of the Sea offers the finest Asian specialties in an elegant setting. Seafood is the specialty. You may hand select your choice of lobster or crab from a 500-gallon aquarium. Chicken, beef, pork, and vegetarian entrées are also available. If seafood strikes your fancy, be sure to stop by and experience the specialties at Pearls of the Sea.

For lighter eating or quick snacks, choose from burgers, deli sandwiches, pizza, Mexican specialties and an assortment of ice cream and desserts at the Bingo Snack Bar. It is located on the second floor in the nonsmoking bingo area. In the casino, try the Sunset Deli, open 24 hours a day for hand-carved deli sandwiches, gourmet salads, and pizza. For your sweet tooth you can enjoy hand-dipped ice cream or cheesecakes. The coffee bar will complete your snack with the usual beverages or a steaming hot cappuccino.

ENTERTAINMENT

The Showcase Theater hosts stage, film, and concert events in a state of the art intimate setting. Recent entertainers have been Mickey Finn, Pilata Corrales with the Allegro Dance Team, and international salsa champions Saloman and Sandra Rivera. Tickets for these shows ranged from $15 to $20.

HOTEL AND RESORT

Singing Hills Resort, which was acquired by the band in 2001, is rated among the top semiprivate golf courses in San Diego County. About three miles from the casino, it lies nestled in 425 acres of lush, picturesque mountain terrain. Guests can enjoy two 18-hole championship golf courses, a challenging par-3 course, 11 tournament-class, night-lighted tennis courts, and all of the amenities of a first class destination resort. The lodge has 102 comfortable guest rooms and mini-suites, conference rooms, hospitality rooms, fine dining and banquet facilities, a swimming pool, and putting greens. All hotel rooms offer views of a golf course, the private putting green, or the swimming pool.

The golf courses have been built to take advantage of the area's natural terrain using the mountains, natural rock outcroppings, and aged oaks and sycamores to add character to individual holes. Golfers are challenged to play amongst numerous lakes and strategically placed bunkers before reaching the well-manicured, undulating greens. The courses have been used for numerous PGA, LPGA, USGA and SCGA tournaments and qualifying rounds, and they provide a challenge for golfers of all levels and ability. The Oak and Willow Glen courses are par 72 and approximately 6,600 yards long (back tees). The Pine Glen executive course plays to about 3,000 yards and is a par 54.

Echo's Restaurant, the Singing Hills Resort premier dining facility, welcomes guests to enjoy a fine continental cuisine. House specialties of choice steaks and prime rib and fresh fish selections are supplemented with fine varieties of wine. The coffee shop overlooking the first tee of Willow Glen Golf Course offers wonderful breakfast and lunch selections as diners watch starting golfers. The bar and lounge, nestled against the courtyard, serves a full selection of beverages, cocktails, and delicious appetizers. For reservations call (800) 457-5568.

Take all the time you want to enjoy Sycuan Casino and Resort before hitting the road again for the next stop along the South Branch. You may wish to spend some time at Singing Hills for golf, tennis, swimming, and comfortable overnight quarters before moving on to Viejas Casino and Turf Club.

Double back through Harbison Canyon to I-8 and head east for Viejas Casino. Turn off onto Willows Road in Alpine after about five miles of freeway driving. Cross over the freeway, and take Willows Road east, running parallel to the freeway for a couple miles through the reservation. The Viejas Casino is on the left, and the Viejas Outlet Center is on the right. These are both exemplary architectural complexes that you should explore and enjoy to the fullest. For shopper's convenience there is parking behind the outlet center. Casino parking is on the opposite side of Willows Road, adjacent to the casino. If you want valet service parking, go to the eastside of the casino, turn left into the side entrance and the parking attendants will assist you.

VIEJAS CASINO AND TURF CLUB

Viejas Casino and Turf Club, 5000 Willows Road, Alpine, CA 91901
Owned and operated by: Viejas Band of the Kumeyaay Nation
Directions: Interstate 8, 35 miles east of San Diego, Willow Road exit
Telephone: (800) 847-6537 toll free
Website: www.viejas.com

Parking: **Valet:** Yes   **Indoor:** No   **Outdoor:** Yes
Bus service: Yes, tour buses, local municipal service
Age for admittance: 18
Player's club: Yes, VIP Rewards Club
Nonsmoking area: Yes
Complimentary nonalcoholic drinks: Yes
Alcoholic beverages: No
Gift shop: Yes
Entertainment: Yes, lounge, showroom, Outlet Center nightly display
Restaurants: Yes, 6: steakhouse, buffet, diner, deli, oriental, snack bar
Casino size/gaming floor: 300,000/100,000 square feet

Table games: 72
Slots & video games: 2,000
Bingo: Yes
Offtrack betting: Yes
Poker room: Yes

Hotel: No
Golf course: No
Special attractions: Retail Outlet Center, RV parks

SUMMARY 21

VIEJAS CASINO AND TURF CLUB

The Viejas Casino and Turf Club is owned and operated by the Viejas Band of the Kumeyaay Nation. Viejas is one of the easiest casinos to find, located on I-8 about 35 miles east of San Diego. The elegant casino and 60-store retail outlet mall illustrate traditional Indian designs with its unusual eye-catching architecture. It is worth seeing for that alone. The attractive complex is on the north side of Interstate 8.

TRIBAL AND CASINO HISTORY

For general Kumeyaay history, see Chapter 1 in this book. For the early history of the Viejas Band, see "Tribal History" in the Barona Valley Ranch Resort and Casino section of this book. The Viejas Band of Kumeyaay Indians has approximately 200 members living on the 1,600-acre Viejas Reservation located in the Viejas Valley east of Alpine. They were originally located by El Capitan Dam on the Capitan Grande Reservation.

The displaced Indians from the Capitan Grande Reservation were given token compensation for their lands. Twenty-eight families, including a few members of the Capitan Grande band who joined the Los Conejos group, purchased the Viejas Valley, which was known as the Baron Long Ranch. They incorporated the name Viejas in the late 1980s. A few other families from the Los Conejos group bought private individual sites with their compensation.

Courtesy Viejas Casino and Turf Club

After the move, the Viejas were denied their water rights, and their valley land became solely dependent on meager supplies of rainfall and ground water.

Today, membership in the Viejas Band of the Kumeyaay Nation is given to direct descendents of the families forced from the Capitan Grande Reservation who pooled their shares of dam site purchase money to buy Viejas Valley.

The Viejas Band's democratic government consists of the general council, which includes all of the band's 167 adult voting members. They elect the tribal chairman, tribal council, and by law, vote on all land use decisions. Three council members and the tribal chairman, vice chairman, secretary, and treasurer are elected for two-year terms of office. The tribal council governs tribal activities and makes law, with the approval of the general membership, acting as the executive, legislative, and judicial branches of government. The tribal council also serves as the board of directors for the band's economic enterprises.

A look at the Viejas tribal officers quickly dispels old stereotypes of Hollywood Indians. A good example is the chairman of the Viejas Band, Anthony R. Pico, who has been a worthy leader of his people as well as an effective modern-day executive. A Vietnam veteran paratrooper, he is respected nationally for his initiative in developing Indian gaming and having the vision and determination to lead his people to self-sufficiency. Although the band is relatively small, they are not short of trained executives to manage this $50 million business nor are they dependent solely on male leadership. Three of the seven tribal officers are women.

The Viejas Band embarked on its first free enterprise venture, Ma-Tar-Awa (great open space), a recreational vehicle park, in 1975. The success of this venture provided funds and experience to undertake the more ambitious project of a gaming casino. Helped by enabling legislation, the casino prospered.

The first casino opened in 1991 with 100,000 square feet and 350 employees. Expansion completed in 1999 brought the total footage of the casino and administrative quarters to about 300,000 square feet. Currently, there are more than 2,200 employees with a payroll of over $40 million per year.

Only a few years ago, Viejas Reservation unemployment was as high as 80 percent. Sixty percent of the housing was substandard. Today, as a result of revenues from tribal government gaming, there is no unemployment. The band has built new homes, improved older residences, expanded the tribal government center, constructed a community park, a fire station, a senior citizens' center, and otherwise provided for the health and well being of tribal members. In addition, the band has embarked on a multimillion dollar series of environmental projects to restore the reservation land, watershed, streams and wetlands.

Success in Indian gaming provided funds for other investments, including the $35 million outlet center, another RV park, and the purchase of majority interest in the Borrego Springs Bank. Plans to expand Viejas enterprises beyond San Diego County were disclosed in October 2002 when *The San Diego Union-Tribune* reported that "Viejas announced an unprecedented partnership with three other tribes and a Washington, D.C., developer to build a $43 million Marriott hotel, three blocks from the nation's Capitol."[30]

GAMES

The casino is equipped with 2,000 of the most popular electronic video games and slots and 72 tables for poker, Pai Gow, baccarat, blackjack, Viejas stud, and Hold'Em. A special feature of Viejas is the 350-seat offtrack betting facility, where races can be viewed and bets made on horse races from tracks across the country. There is also a very active 1,200-seat bingo hall. Nonsmoking sections are provided in the gaming areas.

Popular slots, of reel type (with pull handles) and video machines of the widest variety in denominations from 1¢ to $100, can be found throughout the casino floor. Spinning reel machines, such as Double Diamond®, Triple Diamond®, Red, White & Blue®, and Sizzling 7s®, the favorites of die-hard slot players, are available in abundance.

Video poker games of single and multiple hands of many denominations give players a chance to demonstrate their poker skills by selecting the best cards to build a poker hand. For the video game enthusiasts, all the favorites games in the latest versions, from Wheel of Fortune®, Monopoly®, I Dream of Jeanie™, and Yahtzee®, can be found at Viejas.

A new 16,000 square foot gaming room gives video gaming enthusiasts the feeling they are in a huge outdoor canyon surrounded by large rock walls. Overhead a curved ceiling with a sunset streaked sky leads the viewer's eyes to a dome shaped starry night sky.

For blackjack players, there are plenty of tables taking bets up to $3,000 per hand. Blackjack tournaments are held on Tuesdays and Saturdays. For more details about tournaments, call (800) 84 POKER and ask for a floor person. No club points are awarded for tournament play. Viejas policy is that only English can be spoken at blackjack tables.

The VIP Rewards Club is the Viejas player's club for accumulating valuable points while gaming. Ask directions from the first security person you see as you enter the casino for the registration area. Each 100 points accumulated is worth $1 purchasing power at restaurants, or it can be used for entertainment tickets, gift shop items, or gift certificates for friends. This is a more generous ratio than found at many other casinos. The VIP card will also reward you with extra discounts at the Viejas Outlet Center.

Bingo players feel at home at Viejas in the comfortable bingo hall, which is equipped with easy to view large displays. Handheld units and computer setups are available. Bingo is played seven days a week with sessions at 11 a.m., 2 p.m., 6:30 p.m. (earlybird), and 7 p.m. The regular nightly session begins at 7 p.m., Monday though Saturday. Buy-ins are $11 for 12 cards, making you eligible to win $1,000 prizes. On Sunday the sessions are at noon and 4:30 p.m. Sunday buy-ins are $16 for 12 cards, making you eligible to win $1,500 prizes. The popular senior special, held on Monday, Wednesday, and Friday, is a $2.50 buy-in.

RESTAURANTS

Viejas Casino's Executive Chef Gary Legg manages one of the largest kitchens in southern California, serving over 5,000 meals every day. Gary is always looking for appetizing new additions to please diners. By operating their own in-house butcher shop and bakery, Viejas guarantees absolute freshness and also keeps operating costs down, a savings they pass on to casino guests. One shining example is the new Sterling Silver Beef program for the Grove Steakhouse, which brings outstanding premium quality steaks to the table at reasonable prices. "Diners at Viejas are in a win-win situation because 90 percent of everything we serve is prepared right here," says Legg.[31]

Critics and steak lovers alike are raving about the Grove Steakhouse with its fabulous selection of great steaks, seafood, chops, amazing desserts and more. The neighborly prices keep patrons coming back. Lunch hours are 11 a.m. to 4 p.m. everyday. Dinner hours are 4:30 p.m. to 10 p.m. Sunday through Thursday, and 4:30 p.m. to 11:00 p.m. Friday and Saturdays. Reservations are available by calling toll free (800) 847-6537 — ask for ext. 2838. The Grove also provides an elegant ambience with its spacious 100-seat cocktail lounge nestled against a shimmering wall décor.

For a bountiful feast of great food choices the 350-seat Harvest Buffet has it all, from soup to nuts, and everything imaginable in between. The spacious airy surroundings with floor to ceiling natural light puts diners in a relaxed mood and provides a great view overlooking scenic Viejas Valley. Diners may choose from an assortment of salads including fresh Caesar salads, "make your own baked potatoes," a variety of appetizing pastas, carving stations, pizzas, "make your own tacos," and fresh breads and desserts. Lunch is served from 11 a.m. to 4 p.m. The lunch buffet is $7.99 per person. Dinner is served from 4 p.m. to 9:30 p.m. on Sunday through Thursday and from 4 p.m. to 11 p.m. on Friday and Saturday. The dinner buffet is $9.99 per person. Sunday brunch is served from 9 a.m. to 4 p.m. for $13.99 per person. Special pricing for children 12 years and under is $3.99 for lunch, $4.99 for dinner, and $7.99 for Sunday brunch. Every Tuesday and Wednesday crab and shrimp are featured at an additional cost.

Chef Tom Fat of China Camp, famous in downtown San Diego, brings his delicious foods to the East County. He offers the finest in Chinese food at the China Camp Express from 11 a.m. to 2 a.m. to satisfy both the day and night crowd — even the late night owls.

The Sunrise Diner with its 1950s décor is the place to order hamburgers and fries and other fast foods. It is open 24 hours except on Tuesdays from midnight to 7 a.m. when it is closed for cleaning.

The Mezz Deli and Lounge is a casual place for around the clock drinks and dining, from a wide variety of appetizers and deli specialty sandwiches, soups, and salads. For others who wish to grab a quick bite, the casino offers convenience food and drink concessions at the poker bar and bingo snack bar.

ENTERTAINMENT

The Dream Catcher Show Room features a full-service cocktail lounge, stage, dance floor, and Las Vegas style seating with sound and lighting technology comparable to any in the region. It offers a variety of entertainment, special concerts, and shows. For larger concerts, the park area adjoining the outlet center is used. Top name entertainers are featured on a regular basis.

VIEJAS OUTLET CENTER

Borrowing ideas from Southwest pueblo architecture on the ways that Native Americans adapted habitats to the environment, modern-day architects have provided a way to enjoy a beautiful natural-like setting as shoppers stroll among the 60 retail outlet stores. This unique presentation combines the utility of adjoining stores with a feeling of being in the great outdoors. The Viejas Outlet Center has won numerous awards for its architecture, lighting, and creative design, such as the "Gold Nugget" Award, an "Orchid" from the Orchids & Onions Design Awards, and the THEA Award for themed entertainment properties.

Courtesy Viejas Casino and Turf Club

Viejas Outlet Center looking towards show court

The major foot-traffic link between the casino and outlet center is through the Show Court, located on the periphery of the retail shops. It was designed to recreate a ceremonial ground where elders once sat underneath a shelter and told stories around a campfire. The stage is housed under a large tent-like structure made of massive logs created to look like natural elements. Flamed granite in the center symbolizes an ancient fire pit. Within a 50-foot circle, numerous nozzles emit fountains of soaring waters in tune with background music. In the evening the show is enhanced with lasers and fiery flames that jet 50 feet into the air.

This free showplace is a perfect spot for shoppers and gaming customers to relax and be entertained after a full day of activities. Around the Show Court are several convenience food restaurants for quick meals or snacks.

BUS SERVICE

Viejas welcomes group tours and will provide free bus transportation for groups of 35 people or more from the greater San Diego region. To make reservations for groups in the southern California region, call (619) 659-1764. To make special arrangements for groups or conventions outside the southern California region, call (800) 847-6537, extension 1764 or 1733.

RECREATIONAL VEHICLE PARKS

For those traveling with an RV and looking for overnight accommodations along with the opportunity to visit the casino and outlet center, Ma-Tar-Awa Recreational Vehicle Park is the answer. It offers a store, clubhouse, swimming pool, spa and laundry. It has 88 full hookups, and can accommodate up to 7,000 people at its campsites. Ma-Tar-Awa is located about one mile from the casino. It has a connecting shuttle bus for the convenience of their campers. Alpine Springs RV Park, located by the east entrance of the reservation on Willows Road, is also owned and operated by the Viejas Band.

OVERNIGHT ARRANGEMENTS

For those looking for rooms to stay overnight, Viejas recommends the Country Inn, just a few miles from the action and excitement of Viejas. Reservations for the Country Inn can be made by calling (619) 445-5800.

When you have enjoyed all that Viejas has to offer and are ready to hit the road, continue east on Willows to the next freeway access to I-8 east. It is about 25 miles to the Golden Acorn Casino and Travel Center. This is a small but very comfortable and friendly casino. Their personnel cater to an ever-growing list of patrons by giving them special attention, and they do everything they can to make their small enterprise attractive. Adjoining the casino is a large, 24-hour, auto-truck service center and mart, which is well stocked for travelers. To the rear is a special area for 16 wheelers with its own gas and diesel pumps and a lounge for tired truckers.

GOLDEN ACORN CASINO AND TRAVEL CENTER

Golden Acorn Casino, 1800 Golden Acorn Way, Campo, CA 91906
Owned and operated by: Campo Band of the Kumeyaay Nation
Directions: Interstate 8, east of San Diego, about 20 minutes beyond
    Viejas, take the Crestwood Road exit
Telephone: (866) 794-6244 toll free
Website: www.goldenacorncasino.com

Parking: **Valet:** Yes   **Indoor:** No   **Outdoor:** Yes
Bus service: No
Age for admittance: 18
Player's club: Yes, Player's Gold Club
Nonsmoking area: Yes
Complimentary nonalcoholic drinks: Yes
Alcoholic beverages: Yes
Gift shop: Yes
Entertainment: No
Restaurants: Yes, 2: full-service grill, snacks
Casino size/gaming floor: 45,000/25,000 square feet

Table games: 13
Slots & video games: 750
Bingo: No
Offtrack betting: No
Poker room: No

Hotel: No
Golf course: No
Special attractions: Convenience store and auto service station, truck
    refueling and trucker's lounge

SUMMARY 22

GOLDEN ACORN CASINO AND TRAVEL CENTER

The Golden Acorn Casino, located on the Campo Indian Reservation, is owned and operated by the Campo Band of the Kumeyaay Nation. From its perch overlooking Interstate Highway 8, about 50 miles east of San Diego, it has a commanding view west toward San Diego County and east toward Imperial County. Its unique appeal is its support for travelers, especially long-haul truckers.

TRIBAL AND CASINO HISTORY

See Chapter 1 for the early history of the Kumeyaay. The Campo reservation was established in 1893. Through the years the Campo Band has been striving for economic self-support. In 1978 they designated the area near the interstate for economic development. Through the 1980s they looked at many possible projects for the area, but for lack of financing and business viability they were not pursued.

When the logjam was finally broken for Indian gaming in the 1990s, this option became their central focus. Their approach to a casino business was the subject of much study to assure a project with good prospects for business success and one for which they could get financing. In August 2001 the Golden Acorn Casino opened its doors to the public, and it has being going strong since then.

Courtesy Golden Acorn Casino and Travel Center

According to Mike Connolly, historian for the Campo Band:

> The Campo Kumeyaay must still live with the effects of long time poverty, disrupted families, educational challenges and health impacts. The Campo people have shown their resilience over the ages, and their willingness to rise to the challenges before them. With the Golden Acorn Casino as one critical element, the Campo people will move ahead toward a brighter future for themselves and their children.[32]

The Golden Acorn Casino is a modest structure of about 45,000 square feet that sits just off the freeway. Its 75-foot sign can be seen from either direction. It is located where the air is very clean in the high desert terrain, about 4,000 feet above sea level. It tends to be cooler than other parts of San Diego County, dropping to near freezing on winter evenings with some occasional light snowfall. In warmer months the wind tends to moderate the hot desert climate. To the right of the casino is the convenience store and auto service area, and to the rear of the property on the east side is the trailer truck area.

From the early stages of planning, the Campo Band's executive committee decided to focus on providing more than the usual services for travelers and to provide special facilities for truckers. The San Diego area as a whole has little in the way of truck stops where big rigs can refuel and drivers can rehabilitate. The Golden Acorn Casino on I-8 is now a welcome haven for the men and women who haul cargo on our country's highways.

An advantage of a small casino is the opportunity to develop a closer relationship with customers. Golden Acorn personnel are well aware of this being among their advantages, and they make the best of it.

The Campo Reservation is governed by the tribal council consisting of all adult members, 18 years and older. An executive committee of elected members executes policy and resolutions passed by the general council. In the 2000 elections, Ralph Goff was named chairman. He and the other elected council members serve a four-year term. They have hired a management team that oversees the daily operations of the Casino.

GAMES

Golden Acorn Casino offers 750 of the latest video poker, video keno and video slot machines, including $1,000,000 Pyramid™, American Bandstand®, The Addam's Family™, Austin Powers™, Diamond Cinema™, I Dream of Jeanie™, Ripley's Believe it or Not®, and many more in a wide range of denominations. There are 46 video poker games with denominations of 25¢ to $1 including many progressive machines. For keno players there are 10 machines to choose from.

There's plenty of action and fun at the 13 table games. You can play $2 blackjack and $10 double deck, Pai Gow Poker, 3-card poker, or Let It Ride®. Table limits vary but won't scare off novice players or dissatisfy experienced players. Golden Acorn Casino is the perfect place for those new to table games to get their feet wet without being intimidated. Courteous attendants will help with the rules and break in those uncertain about the games.

Join their Player's Gold Club to earn points good for promotions, cash back, food and merchandise. The Player's Gold Club offers one of the highest point value systems around, 1 point for every $4 wagered.

RESTAURANT

What the casino lacks in numbers of restaurants, it makes up in food varieties, specials, and service. The Golden Grill, open 24 hours a day, is worth the trip for its specials of $7.99 prime rib on Monday, $6.99 T-bone steak platter on Tuesdays and Thursdays, $4.99 Parmesan chicken on Wednesday, and $9.99 steak and lobster on Fridays. Service is from 4-10 p.m. Prices for other menu items are also inviting. Full-service breakfast, lunch, and dinner meals are served nonstop, always with courteous and prompt service. The cuisine is diverse with Asian, Mexican, and Italian entrees along with traditional American foods. For those more on the go, there is counter service for sandwiches, pizza, desserts, and coffee specialties. Customers of all ages are welcome in the restaurant. Gift items can also be purchased at the restaurant checkout counter.

QUICK MART AND TRAVEL CENTER

The auto service center offers all gasoline grade fuels, diesel and a wide variety of food, snacks, and beverages to customers just stopping off from the freeway or enjoying the casino. For truckers there is a separate fueling area with 96 spaces and plenty of room to maneuver and park their rigs. They are invited to relax in the trucker's lounge, watch TV, take a shower, or use the laundry facilities. Customers who purchase $75 or more in diesel fuel are offered a "pay $5 get $10" coupon using the Player's Gold Club card — limit one coupon per day.

After visiting the Golden Acorn Casino and Travel Center it may be time to reconnoiter. The next stop, the Paradise Casino in Winterhaven, is about a two hour drive to the east at the Arizona border. Winterhaven, California, and Yuma, Arizona, are side by side at the Colorado River and are well known as places for retirees and "snowbirds," the seasonal visitors who come from as far north as Canada, to enjoy the relative winter warmth.

PARADISE CASINO

Paradise Casino, 450 Quechan Drive, Winterhaven, CA 92283, and Yuma, AZ

Owned and operated by: Fort Yuma Quechan Indians

Directions: Interstate 8, 180 miles east of San Diego, take the 4th Avenue bridge left to Quechan Drive

Telephone: (760) 572-7777

Website: www.paradisecasinoyuma.com

Parking: **Valet:** No   **Indoor:** No   **Outdoor:** Yes

Bus service: Tour only

Age for admittance: 21

Player's club: Yes, Club Paradise

Nonsmoking area: No

Complimentary nonalcoholic drinks: No

Alcoholic beverages: CA no, AZ yes

Gift shop: Yes, AZ

Entertainment: Outdoor concerts AZ

Restaurants: Yes, 1 cafeteria AZ

Casino size/gaming floor: 45,000/25,000 square feet

Table games: 20 CA, 8 AZ

Slots & video games: 200 CA, 475 AZ

Bingo: Yes AZ

Offtrack betting: No

Poker room: Yes (on the AZ side)

Hotel: No

Golf course: No

Special attractions: Colorado River activities, historic old Yuma, Fort Yuma Quechan Museum

SUMMARY 23

PARADISE CASINO

The Paradise Casino, owned and operated by the Fort Yuma Quechan Indians on the California side of the Arizona border, opened in December 2002. The Paradise Casino of Yuma, Arizona, a scant 20 feet away, has been operating since 1994. The street approach to the casinos on Quechan Drive crosses the border, and the casino entrances are side-by-side. Patrons can enter either the California or the Arizona casino from the parking lot. The casinos are not connected internally.

TRIBAL HISTORY

For the early history of the Quechan, see Chapter 1 in this book. The Quechan Indians are an independent Indian tribe of long standing in this state and national border area. In modern times prior to gaming, the tribe economy was mainly based on agriculture. A substantial annual income of $5 million is generated from the leasing of about 9,000 acres of land to a non-Indian corporation for sand and gravel use. The corporation employs about 10 tribal members. An additional 700 acres have been leased to a non-Indian farmer. In addition to two casinos, the tribe also manages five RV parks, a grocery store, a museum, a fish and game enterprise, and a seasonal parking lot in Andrade for entry into Algodones in Baja California. Quechan enterprises are under the direction of the tribal council headed by Chairman Mike Jackson.

Courtesy Paradise Casino

CASINOS AND GAMES

In southern California we have noted that the Agua Caliente tribe operates two casinos, but the Quechan are the first to operate two in different states, and they may in the future build another California casino adjacent to Interstate 8. The Arizona casino first became engaged in gambling in 1994 with a 300-seat bingo hall in Yuma. This casino backs up to the California border. A few years later they added 475 slots and eight poker tables. The California casino, which is also known as Paradise, is required by law to be separated by 20 feet from the Yuma casino. In the new California Paradise Casino, there is an additional 200 slots and 20 table games, mostly for blackjack since the game is illegal in Arizona. They offer $1 blackjack in addition to the high stakes games. The casino is set below the grade of the road and is attractively decorated with orange and blue accents on sand-colored walls. The interior has a whimsical marine décor with seahorses and seashells. The bingo hall is on the Arizona side and has sessions every evening about 6 p.m. The Arizona side also has a poker room.

RESTAURANT

There is one restaurant on the Arizona side. It has cafeteria service for breakfast, lunch, dinner, and snacks. It is open seven days a week around the clock and prices are very reasonable.

ENTERTAINMENT

Concerts are held in an outdoor amphitheater on a scheduled basis. Call (760) 572-7777 for details.

BUS SERVICE

There is no municipal bus service that stops at the casinos. However, special arrangements can be made for tour buses.

MUSEUM

The Fort Yuma Quechan Museum is housed in a small pink adobe across from the casino and near tribal offices. It is open weekly from 8 a.m. to 5 p.m. and on Saturdays from 10 a.m. to 4 p.m. There is a $1 admission fee, and children under 12 years of age are free. The museum displays artifacts and photos of the tribe and has a small gift shop where native hand crafts can be purchased. Call (760) 572-0661 for information.

NOTES

[1] David J. Valley, *Gaijin Shogun, Gen. Douglas MacArthur, Stepfather of Postwar Japan*, San Diego: Sektor Co, 2000.

[2] Myra Ann DeSomber, "Changing Play Patterns Among the Kumeyaay Diegueño Indians," Master's thesis, San Diego State University, 1975, pp. 32-48.

[3] Katherine Luomala, "Tipai-Ipai" in Robert F. Heizer, ed., *Handbook of North American Indians*, Vol. 8: California, Washington, DC: Smithsonian Institution, 1978, p. 605.

[4] "Indian power grab," *The San Diego Union-Tribune*, August 27, 2002, p. B6.

[5] Las Vegas Investment Advisors, Inc., *Client Services Bulletin*, March 15, 2001, p. 4.

[6] *Barona Casino Journal*, Vol. 13, November, 2000, p. 1.

[7] See Florence Connolly Shipek, *Pushed into the Rocks*, Lincoln, NE: University of Nebraska Press, 1988.

[8] Virginia Bridge Landis, *Handbook on the Indians of Southern California*, San Diego: Museum of Man, 1992, pp. 4-8.

[9] Fr. William Hughes, *Indian Sentinel* 1910, Bureau of Catholic Indian Missions, records collection, Series 4-1, Box 1, Folder 13, Marquette University (Milwaukee).

[10] This tar is a high viscosity petroleum product that oozed upward from the many oil deposits in the Santa Barbara Channel area. The famous La Brea Tar Pits were formed from large masses of this same material.

[11] Robert F. Heizer, ed., *Handbook of North American Indians*, p. 512.

[12] T.B. Sutherland, *The Native American Handbook*, Riverside, CA: Four Directions Press, 2001, as cited in www.fourdir.com/chemehuevi.htm.

[13] See the website for more Chemehuevi references: www.fourdir.com/chemehuevi.htm

[14] Dolan H. Eargle Jr., *Native California Guide*, p. 213.

[15] Jessica Maxwell, "Inside the Hidden Kingdom," *Audubon Magazine*, Vol. 101 (May-June 1995), pp. 61-69.

[16] U.S. Department of Commerce, Economic Development Administration, *American Indian Reservations and Trust Areas*, Tiller Research Inc., 1996. See also: Jeffrey Scott, www.jeff.scott.tripod.com/Yuma.html; www.cinprograms.org/people/coloradorivr/yuma.html; and Andrew Hedlund and Nicolle Wigham, www.emuseum.mnsu.edu/cultural/northamerica/yuma.html.

[17] *San Diego Union-Tribune*, July, 30, 2002, p. B1.

[18] "Grossmont College Connection: Spring 2003 Class Offered at Barona Museum," *Barona Spirits Speak*, Vol. 2, No. 4 (Fall 2002), p. 3.

[19] Roger Fleming, *Win at Video Poker*, Secaucus, NJ: Carol Publishing Group, 1999. Another recommended book is Stanford Wong's *Professional Video Poker*, La Jolla, CA: Pi Yee Press, 1993.

[20] see www.gamblersanonymous.org/about.html

[21] From a local newspaper as reported by the tribal office of the Santa Ynez Band of Chumash Indians.

[22] "Morongo or Maarringa'," *Malki News* (Fall 2002), pp. 4-5.

[23] See www.valleycenter.com/frontpage/henry

[24] See www.sdnch.com/felicita/history.htm

[25] Committee of LHS, *Legends of Lakeside*, Lakeside, CA: Lakeside Historical Society, 1985, p. 4.

[26] Copy of a news release, Barona Indians, May 22, 2002, p. 2.

[27] San Diego Convention & Visitors Bureau, "Barona Casino," *Official San Diego Casino Guide*, 2002, p. 9.

[28] *Golfweek Magazine*, Special Edition, March 5, 2002.

[29] Copy of a news release, Barona Indians, January 26, 2000, p. 1.

[30] Chet Barfield, "Viejas tribe stunned at arrest of chairman in slaying," *The San Diego Union-Tribune*, October 21, 2002, pp. B1, B4.

[31] Conversation with the author, Barona Casino, June 20, 2002.

[32] "The Struggles and Triumphs of the Campo Kumeyaay Band," *The San Diego Gaming Guide*, Vol. 1 (April 2002), p. 8.

INDEX

SUNBELT PUBLICATIONS

"Adventures in the Natural and Cultural History of the Californias"
Series Editor — Lowell Lindsay

San Diego Series

Rise and Fall of San Diego: 150 Million Years	Abbott
Only in America: The Story of the Alessio Brothers	Alessio
More Adventures with Kids in San Diego	Botello, Paxton
Geology of San Diego: Journeys Through Time	Clifford, Bergen, Spear
Mission Trails Regional Park Trail Map	Cook
Cycling San Diego, 3rd Ed.	Copp, Schad
La Jolla: A Celebration of Its Past	Daly-Lipe, Dawson
A Good Camp: Gold Mines of Julian and the Cuyamacas	Fetzer
San Diego Mountain Bike Guide	Greenstadt
San Diego Specters: Ghosts, Poltergeists, Tales	Lamb
San Diego Padres, 1969-2001: A Complete History (Big League Press)	Papucci
San Diego: An Introduction to the Region, 3rd Ed.	Pryde
San Diego Architecture (SD Architectural Foundation)	Sutro
Campgrounds of San Diego County	Tyler

Southern California Series

Geology Terms in English and Spanish	Aurand
Gateway to Alta California: Expedition to San Diego, 1769	Crosby
Portrait of Paloma: A Novel	Crosby
Orange County: A Photographic Collection	Hemphill
California's El Camino Real and Its Historic Bells	Kurillo, Tuttle
Warbird Watcher's Guide to the Southern California Skies	Smith
Campgrounds of Los Angeles and Orange Counties	Tyler
Campgrounds of Santa Barbara and Ventura Counties	Tyler
Mission Memoirs: Photographs and Reflections on California's Past	Ruscin

California Desert Series

Anza-Borrego A To Z: People, Places, and Things	D. Lindsay
The Anza-Borrego Desert Region (Wilderness Press)	L. Lindsay
Geology of the Imperial/Mexicali Valleys (SDAG 1998)	L. Lindsay, ed.
Palm Springs Oasis: A Photographic Essay	Lawson
Desert Lore of Southern California, 2nd Ed.	Pepper
Peaks, Palms, and Picnics: Day Journeys Coachella Valley	Pyle
Geology of Anza-Borrego: Edge of Creation	Remeika, Lindsay
Paleontology of Anza-Borrego (SDAG 1995)	Remeika, Sturz, eds.
California Desert Miracle: Parks and Wilderness	Wheat

Baja California Series

The Other Side: Journeys in Baja California	Botello
Cave Paintings of Baja California, Rev. Ed.	Crosby
Backroad Baja: The Central Region	Higginbotham
Lost Cabos: The Way it Was (Lost Cabos Press)	Jackson
Journey with a Baja Burro	Mackintosh
Houses of Los Cabos (Amaroma)	Martinez, ed.
Baja Legends: Historic Characters, Events, Locations	Niemann
Loreto, Baja California: First Mission/Capital of Spanish Calif. (Tio Press)	O'Neil
Baja Outpost: The Guest Book from Patchen's Cabin	Patchen
Sea of Cortez Review	Redmond